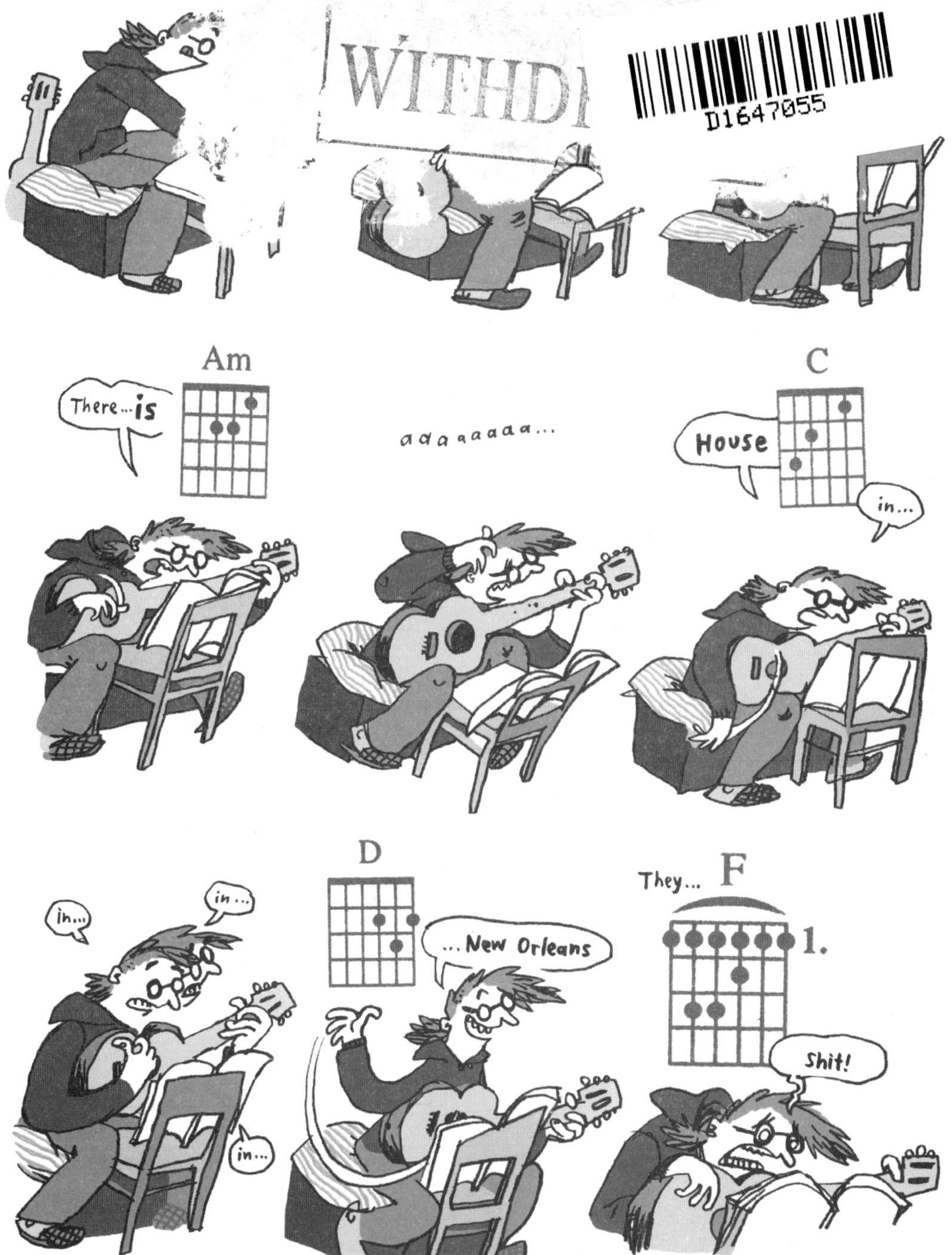
Am
There... is
aaaaaaaa...
C
House
in...
in...
in...
in...
D
... New Orleans
They...
F
1.
Shit!

BLANK SLATE
presents

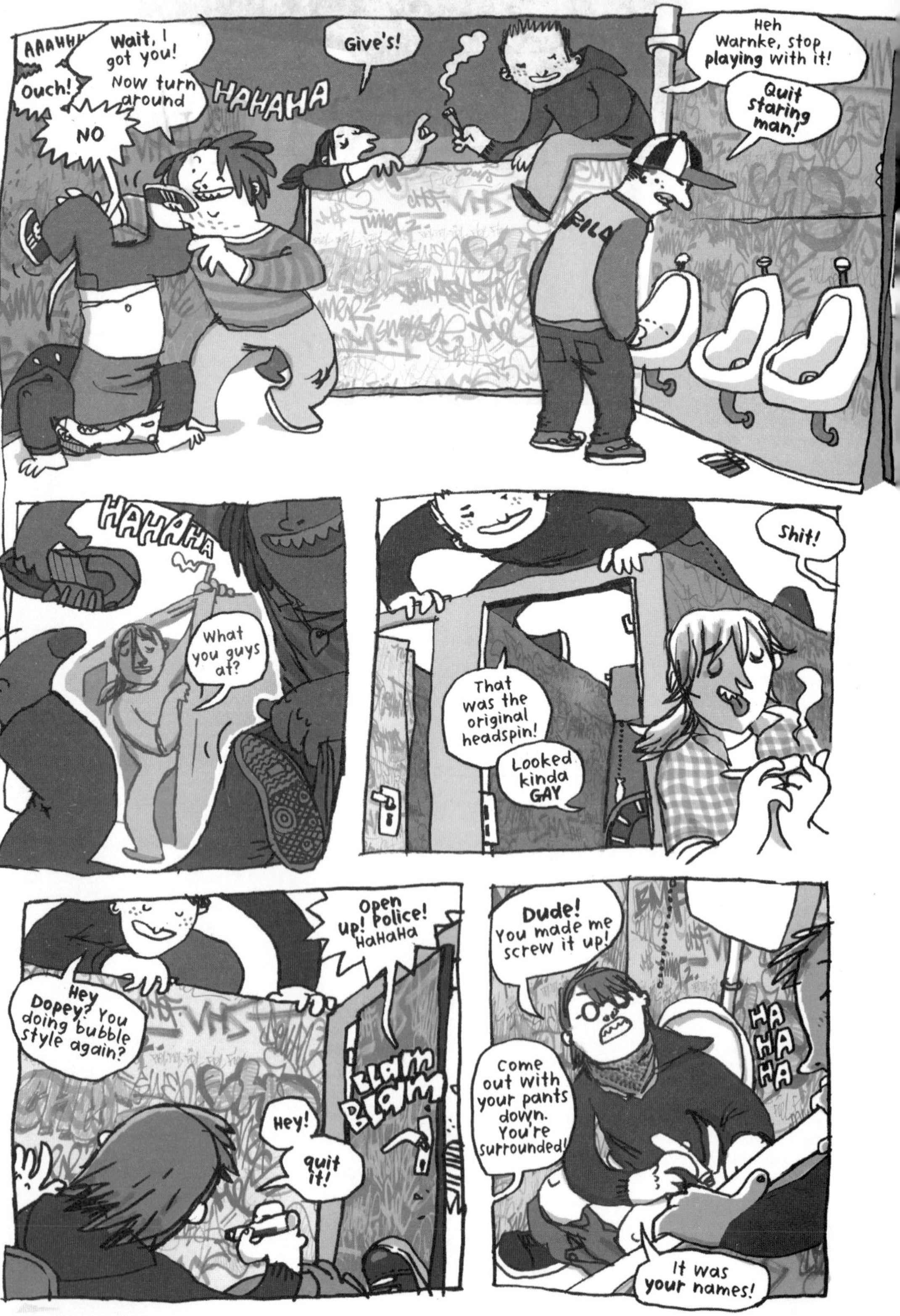
AAAHH
Ouch!
Wait, I got you!
Now turn around
NO
HAHAHA
Give's!
Heh Warnke, stop playing with it!
Quit staring man!
FILA
HAHAHA
What you guys at?
Shit!
That was the original headspin!
Looked kinda GAY
Open up! Police! HaHaHa
Hey Dopey? You doing bubble style again?
BLAM BLAM
Hey!
quit it!
Dude! You made me screw it up!
HA HA HA HA
Come out with your pants down. You're surrounded!
It was your names!

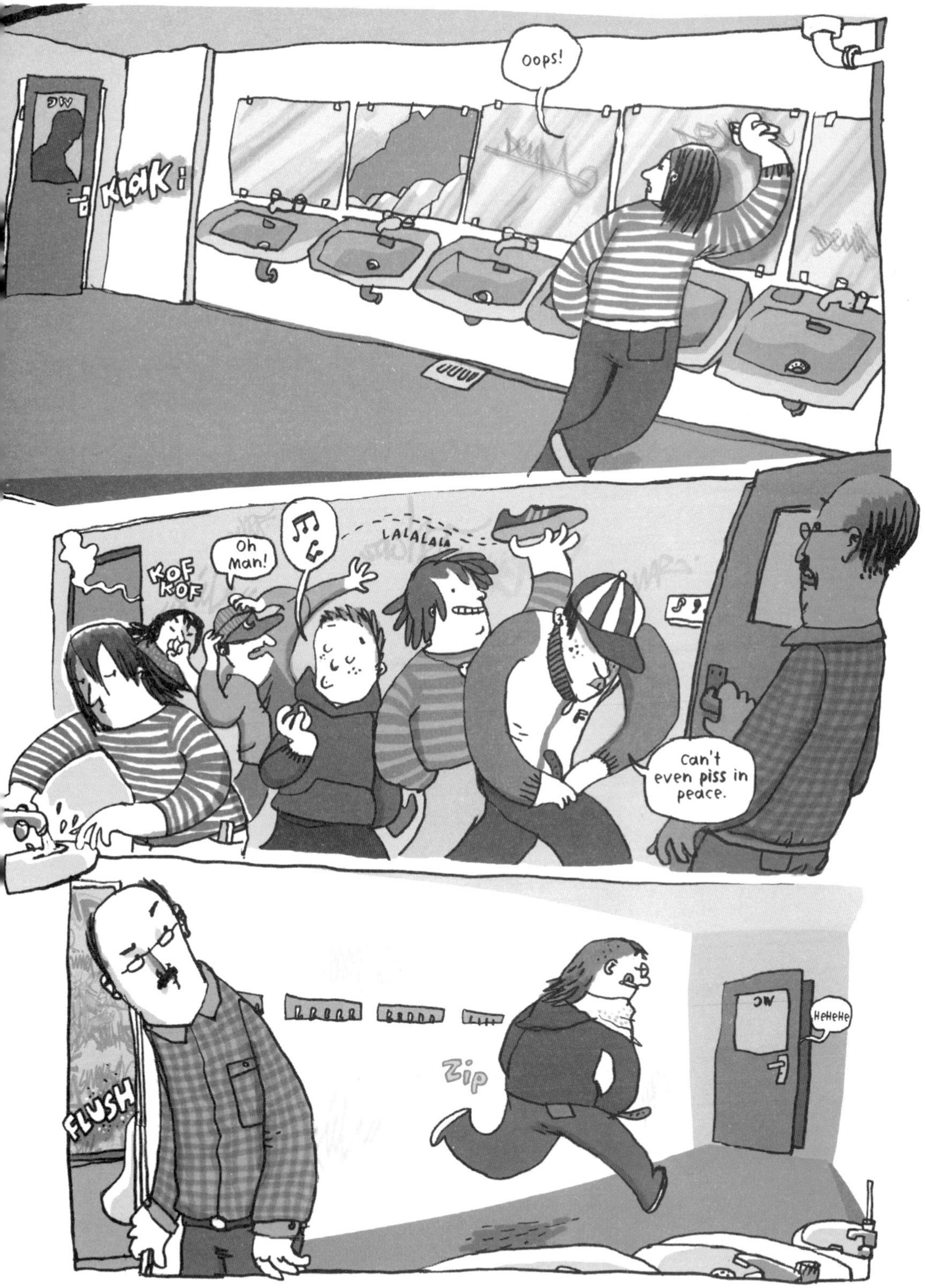
KLAK!
Oops!
KOF KOF
Oh Man!
LALALALA
Can't even piss in peace.
FLUSH
Zip
HeHeHe

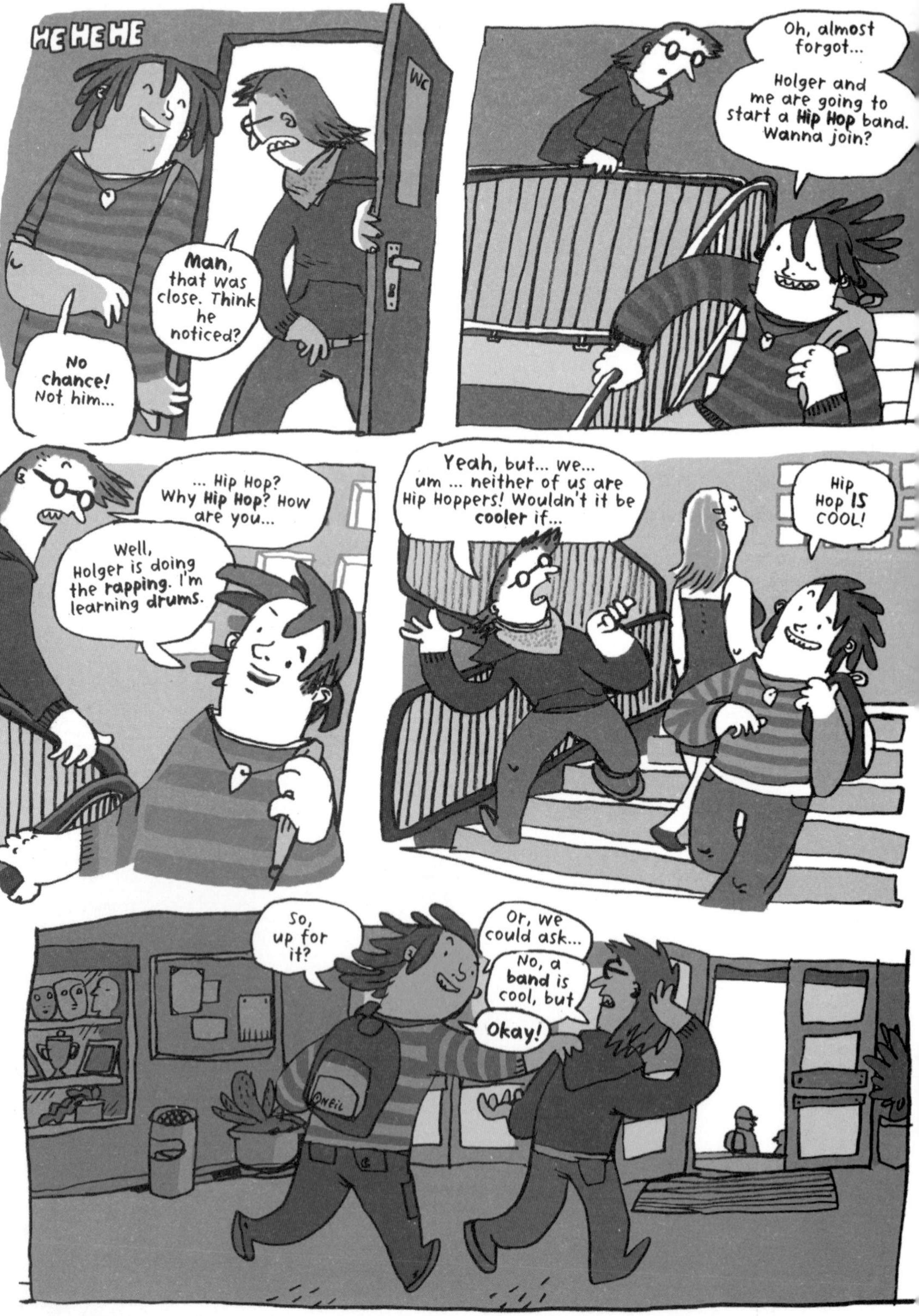

HE HE HE
WC
Man, that was close. Think he noticed?
No chance! Not him...
Oh, almost forgot...
Holger and me are going to start a Hip Hop band. Wanna join?
... Hip Hop? Why Hip Hop? How are you...
Well, Holger is doing the rapping. I'm learning drums.
Yeah, but... we... um ... neither of us are Hip Hoppers! Wouldn't it be cooler if...
Hip Hop IS COOL!
So, up for it?
Or, we could ask...
No, a band is cool, but
Okay!
O'NEIL

THE BAND

ISBN 978-1-906653-156
Publisher: kenny Penman
Group Editor and Translator: Isobel Rips
Editorial Assistant: Martin Steenton & Judith Taboy
Publishers Assistant & Marketing: Kayla Marie Hillier

First published by Reprodukt, Berlin 2004
First English Edition Blank Slate Books, London 2011

keep up with mawil at
www.mawil.net

Discover more about Blank Slate at
www.BlankSlateBooks.co.uk

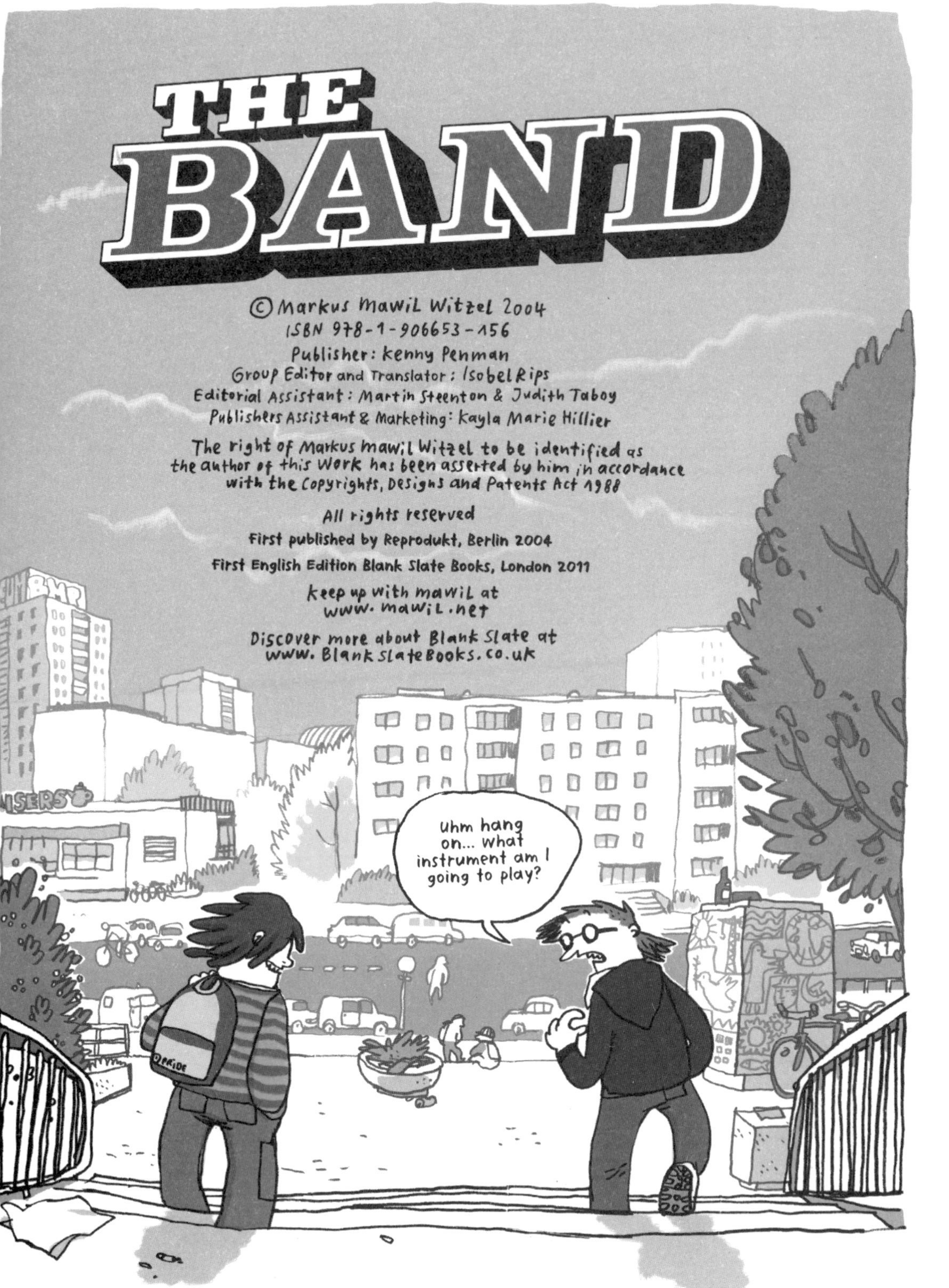
uhm hang on... what instrument am I going to play?

SVEN WASN'T REALLY A HIP HOPPER. HE GAVE ME MY FIRST BOB MARLEY ALBUM AND 'NEVERMIND'. HE HELPED ME BUY MY FIRST PAIR OF DOCS AND AT FIRST THOUGHT GRAFFITI WAS CHILDISH

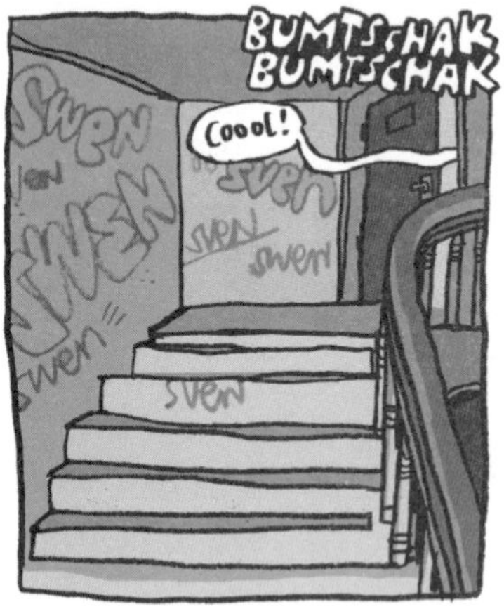
BUMTSCHAK
BUMTSCHAK
Coool!
SVEN
SVEN
SVEN
SVEN
sven
sven
sven

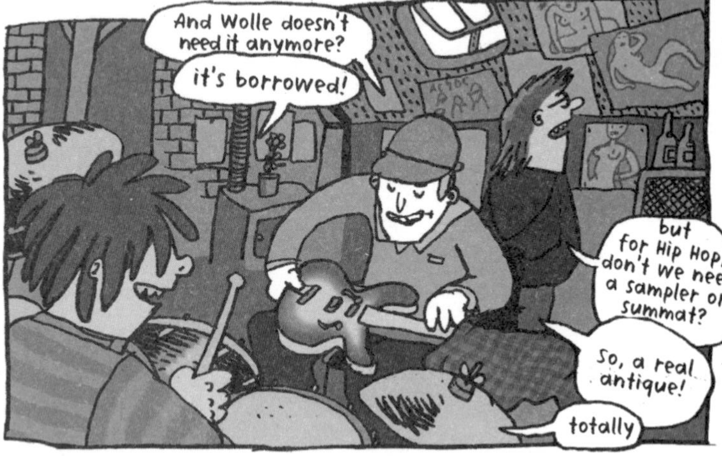
And Wolle doesn't need it anymore?
it's borrowed!
but for Hip Hop, don't we need a sampler or summat?
So, a real antique!
totally

WILD ORCHID, ONE OF THE LAST FEW PROPER METAL BANDS (AT OUR SCHOOL) LET US USE THEIR ATTIC TO REHEARSE

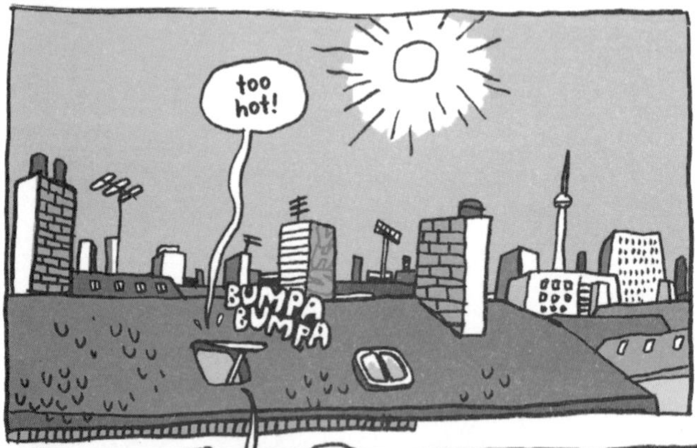
too hot!
BUMPA
BUMPA

THEIR SINGER (A FORMER CHILD ACTOR ON A CHRISTMAS TV SHOW) LIVED ON THE FLOOR BELOW

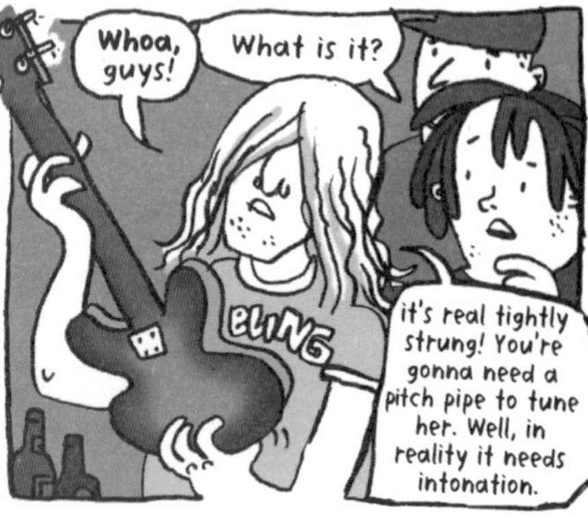
Whoa, guys!
What is it?
BLING
it's real tightly strung! You're gonna need a pitch pipe to tune her. Well, in reality it needs intonation.

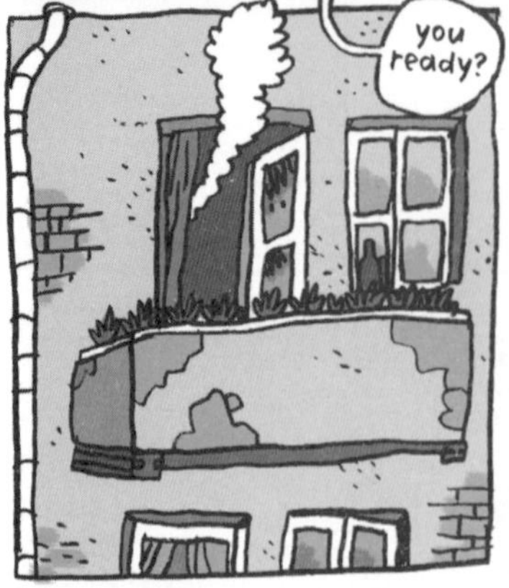
you ready?

THE OTHER FLAT IS WHERE SVEN AND HOLGER'S SWIMMING COACH LIVED. I THINK HE WAS REALLY THEIR DEALER

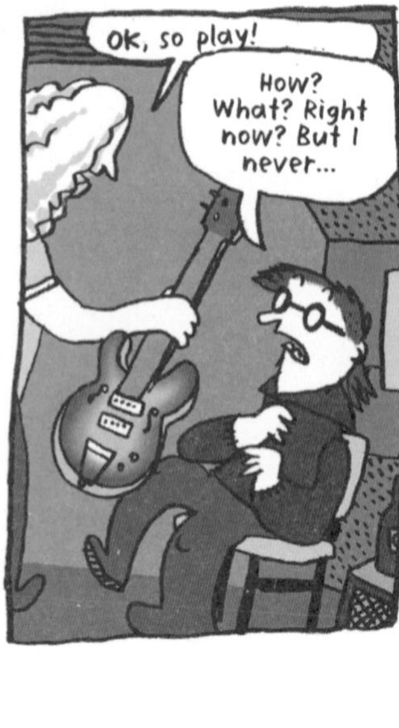
OK, so play!
How? What? Right now? But I never...

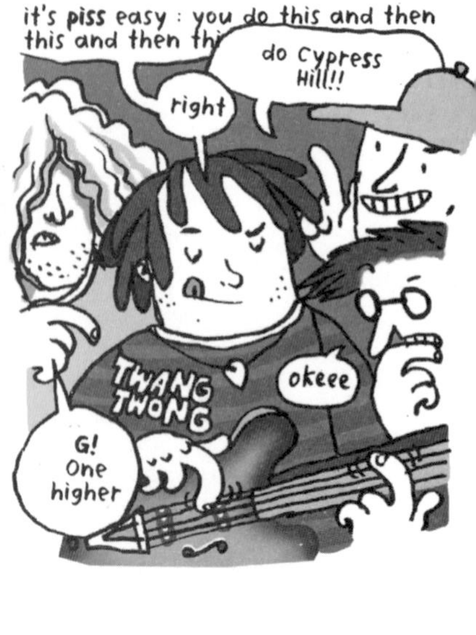
it's piss easy : you do this and then this and then thi
do Cypress Hill!!
right
TWANG
TWONG
okeee
G! One higher

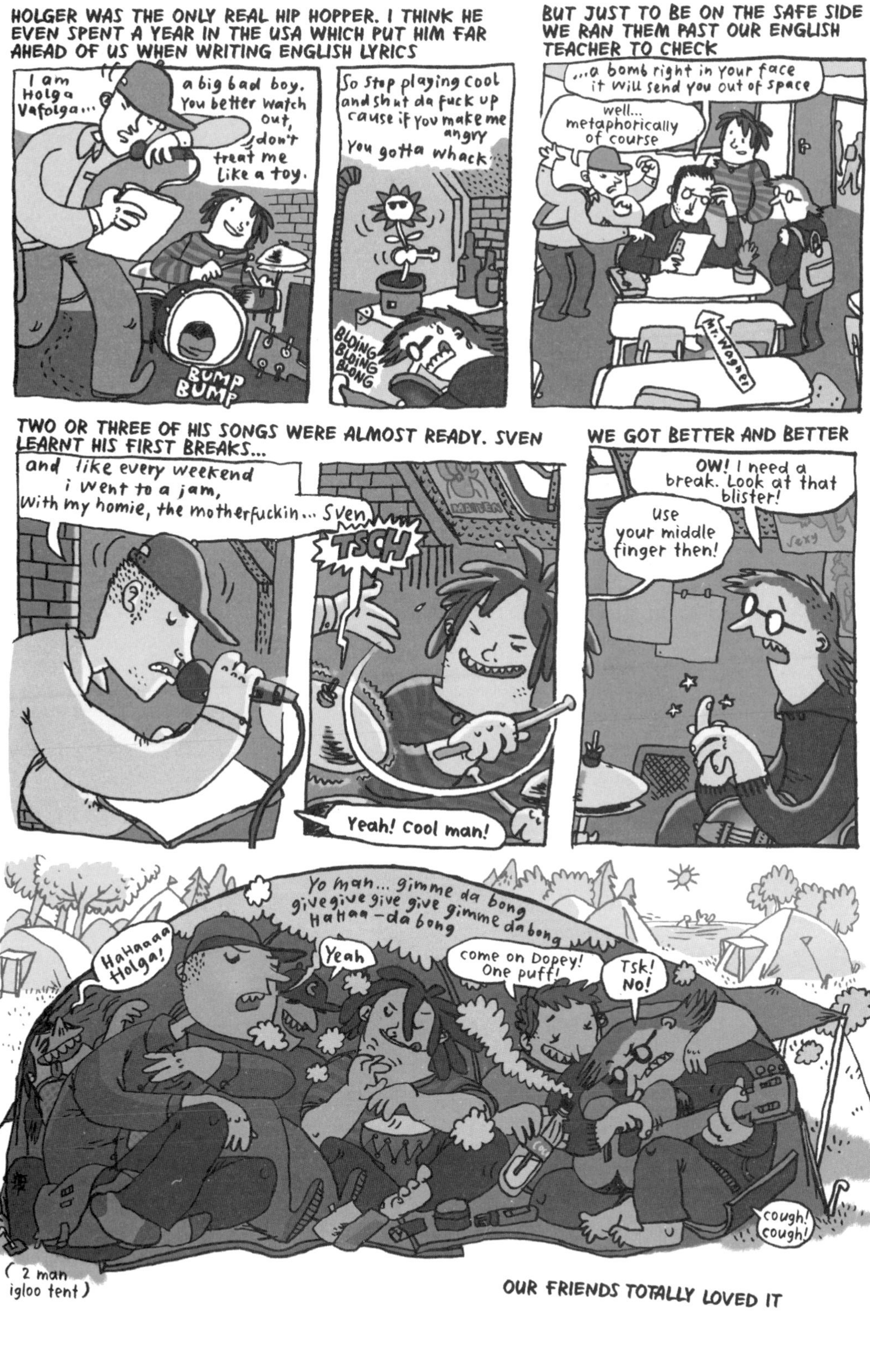
HOLGER WAS THE ONLY REAL HIP HOPPER. I THINK HE EVEN SPENT A YEAR IN THE USA WHICH PUT HIM FAR AHEAD OF US WHEN WRITING ENGLISH LYRICS
I am Holga Vafolga...
a big bad boy. You better watch out, don't treat me like a toy.
BUMP BUMP
So stop playing cool and shut da fuck up cause if you make me angry
You gotta whack
BLOING BLOING BLONG
BUT JUST TO BE ON THE SAFE SIDE WE RAN THEM PAST OUR ENGLISH TEACHER TO CHECK
...a bomb right in your face it will send you out of space
well... metaphorically of course
Mr. Wagner
TWO OR THREE OF HIS SONGS WERE ALMOST READY. SVEN LEARNT HIS FIRST BREAKS...
and like every weekend i went to a jam, with my homie, the motherfuckin... Sven
TSCH
Yeah! Cool man!
WE GOT BETTER AND BETTER
OW! I need a break. Look at that blister!
Use your middle finger then!
Yo man... gimme da bong givegive give give gimme da bong HaHaa-da bong
HaHaaaa Holga!
Yeah
come on Dopey! One puff!
Tsk! No!
cough! cough!
(2 man igloo tent)
OUR FRIENDS TOTALLY LOVED IT

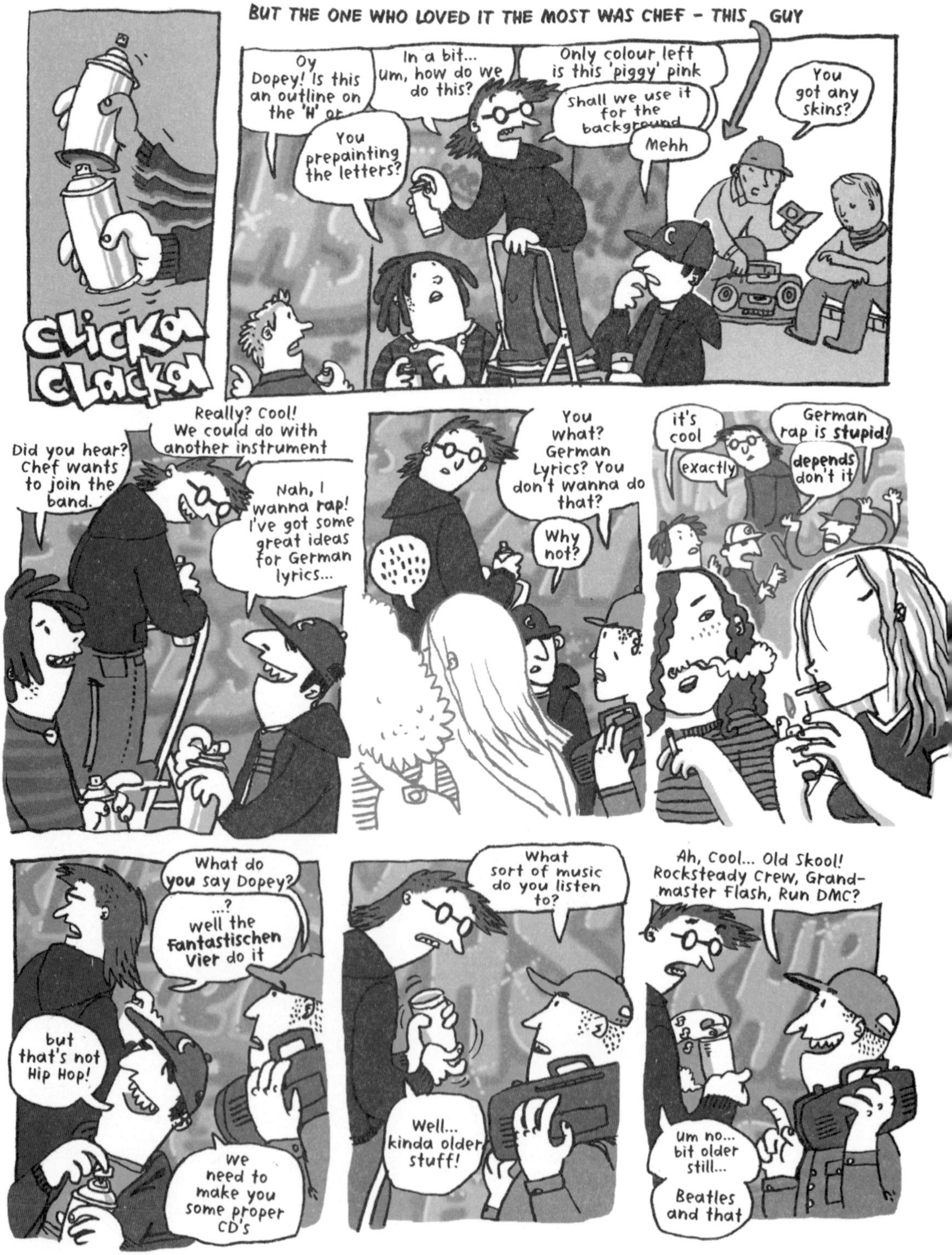
BUT THE ONE WHO LOVED IT THE MOST WAS CHEF - THIS GUY
Clicka Clacka
Oy Dopey! Is this an outline on the 'H' or
You prepainting the letters?
In a bit... um, how do we do this?
Only colour left is this 'piggy' pink
Shall we use it for the background
Mehh
You got any skins?
Did you hear? Chef wants to join the band.
Really? Cool! We could do with another instrument
Nah, I wanna rap! I've got some great ideas for German lyrics...
You what? German Lyrics? You don't wanna do that?
Why not?
it's cool
exactly
German rap is stupid!
depends don't it
What do you say Dopey?
...? well the Fantastischen Vier do it
but that's not Hip Hop!
we need to make you some proper CD's
What sort of music do you listen to?
Well... kinda older stuff!
Ah, Cool... Old Skool! Rocksteady Crew, Grand-master Flash, Run DMC?
Um no... bit older still...
Beatles and that

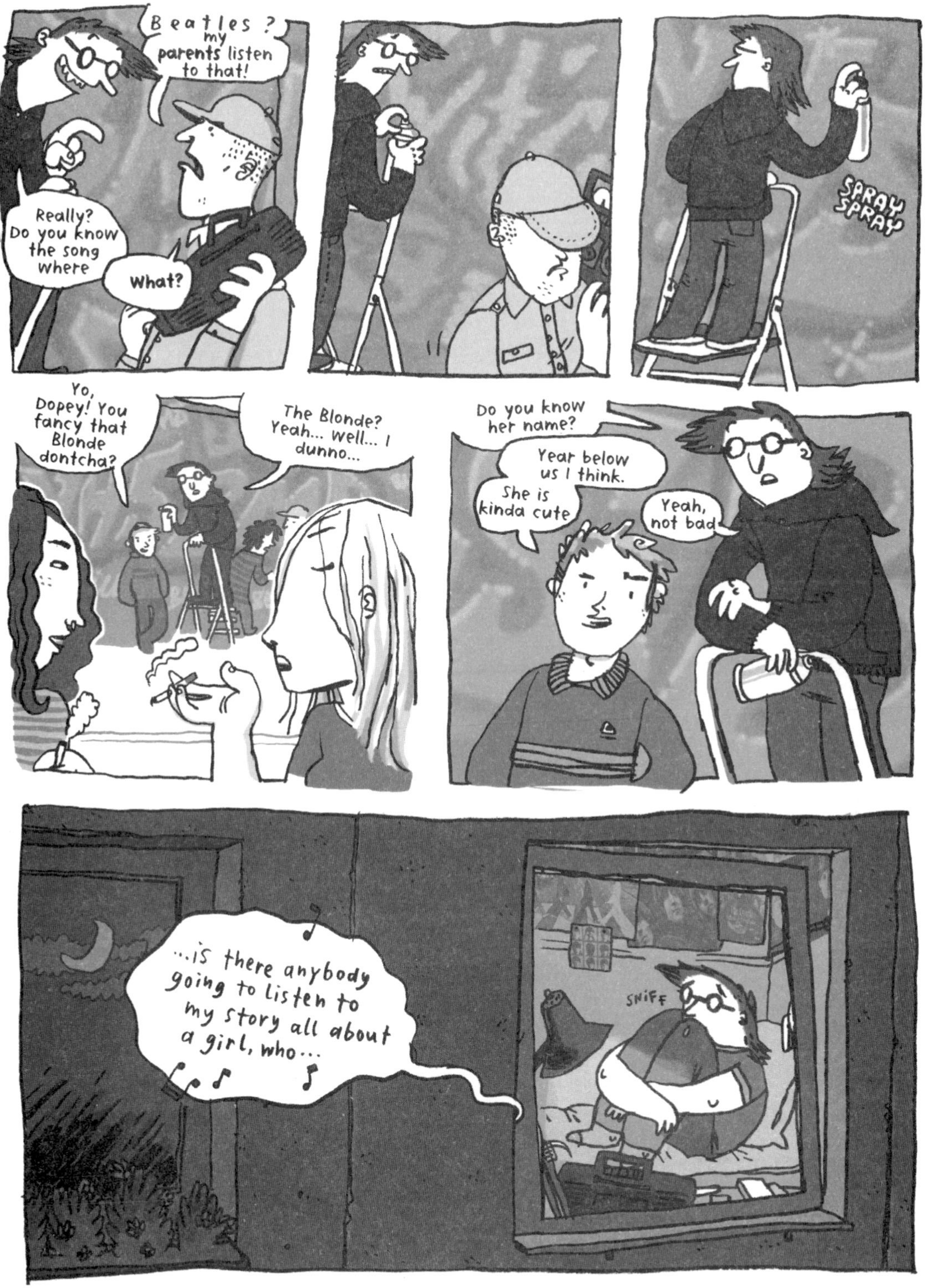
Beatles? my parents listen to that!
Really? Do you know the song where
What?
SPRAY SPRAY
Yo, Dopey! You fancy that Blonde dontcha?
The Blonde? Yeah... well... I dunno...
Do you know her name?
Year below us I think.
She is kinda cute
Yeah, not bad
...is there anybody going to listen to my story all about a girl, who...
SNIFF

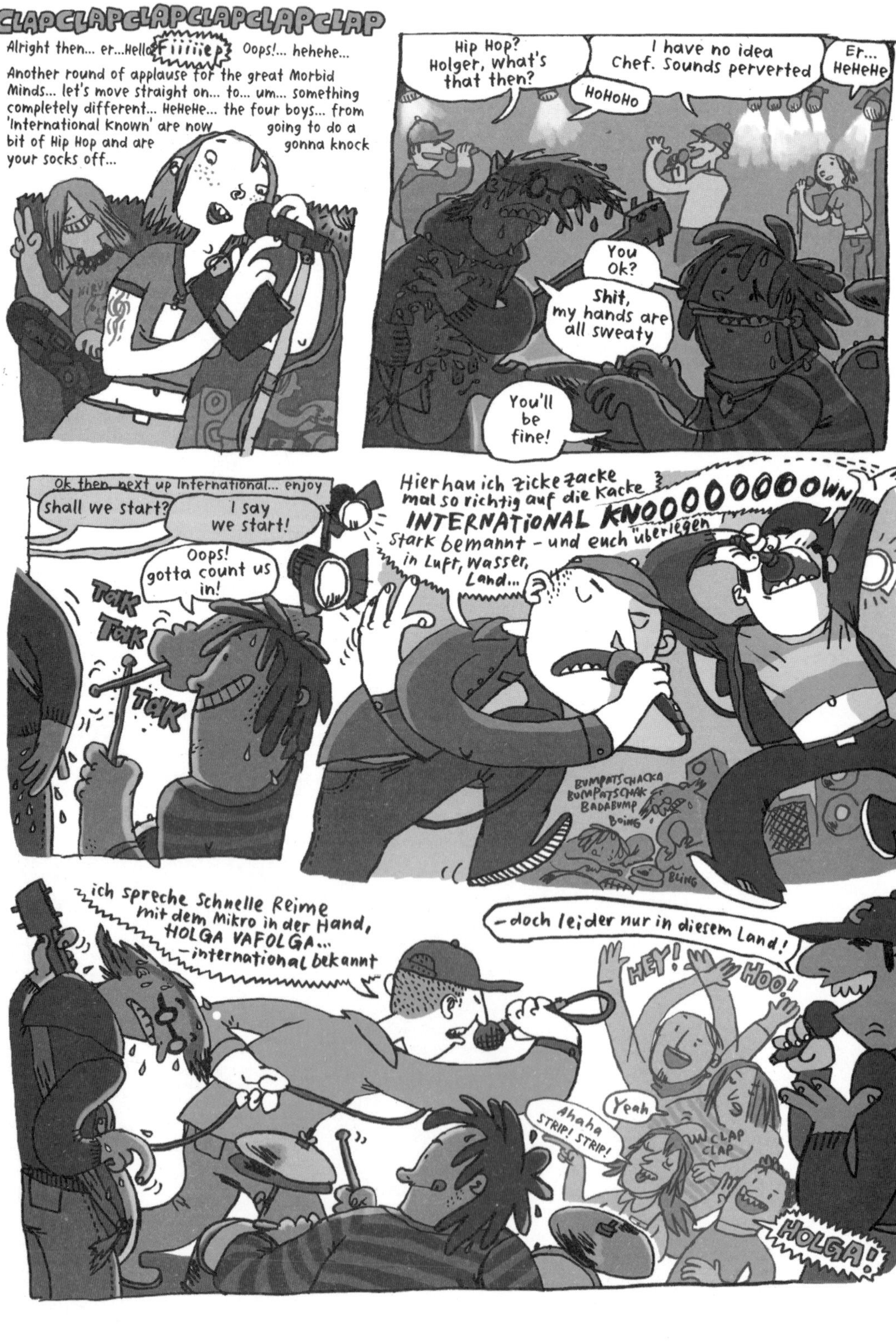
CLAPCLAPCLAPCLAPCLAPCLAP
Alright then... er...Hello Fiiiiiep Oops!... hehehe...
Another round of applause for the great Morbid Minds... let's move straight on... to... um... something completely different... HeHeHe... the four boys... from 'International Known' are now going to do a bit of Hip Hop and are gonna knock your socks off...
Hip Hop? Holger, what's that then?
I have no idea Chef. Sounds perverted
HoHoHo
Er... HeHeHe
You Ok?
Shit, my hands are all sweaty
You'll be fine!
Ok then, next up International... enjoy
Shall we start?
I say we start!
Oops! gotta count us in!
TAK
TAK
TAK
Hier hau ich zicke zacke mal so richtig auf die Kacke
INTERNATIONAL KNOOOOOOOOOWN
Stark bemannt – und euch überlegen in Luft, Wasser, Land...
BUMPATSCHACKA
BUMPATSCHAK
BADABUMP
BOING
BLING
ich spreche schnelle Reime mit dem Mikro in der Hand, HOLGA VAFOLGA... –international bekannt
–doch leider nur in diesem Land!
HEY!
HOO!
Yeah
Ahaha STRIP! STRIP!
CLAP CLAP
HOLGA!

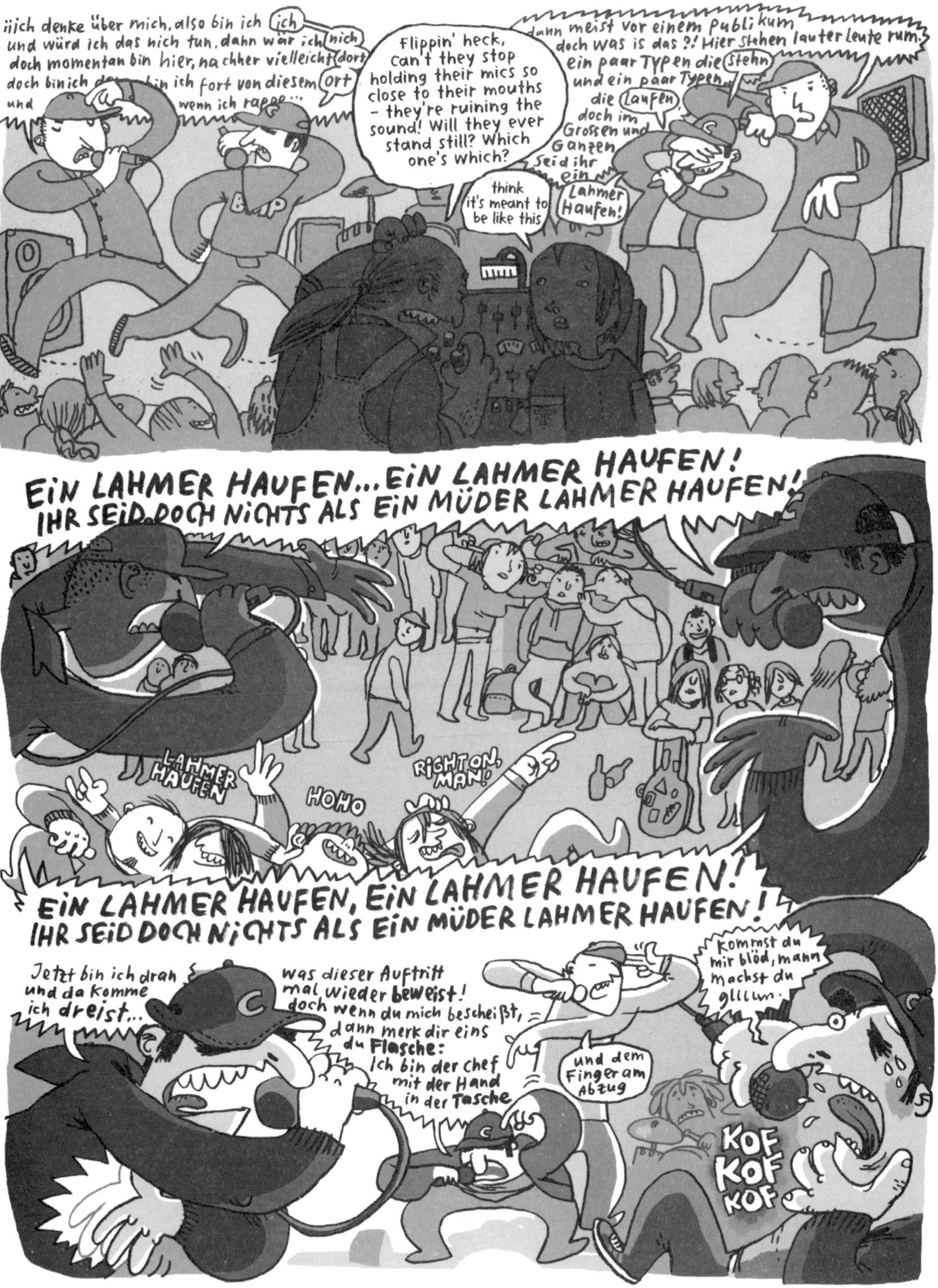

iich denke über mich, also bin ich ich
und würd ich das nich tun, dann wär ich nich
doch momentan bin hier, nachher vielleicht dort
doch bin ich ... bin ich fort von diesem Ort
und ... wenn ich rappe...
Flippin' heck, can't they stop holding their mics so close to their mouths – they're ruining the sound! Will they ever stand still? Which one's which?
think it's meant to be like this
dann meist vor einem Publikum
doch was is das ?! Hier stehen lauter Leute rum.
ein paar Typen die stehn
und ein paar Typen...
die laufen,
doch im Grossen und Ganzen Seid ihr ein
Lahmer Haufen!
EIN LAHMER HAUFEN... EIN LAHMER HAUFEN!
IHR SEID DOCH NICHTS ALS EIN MÜDER LAHMER HAUFEN!
LAHMER HAUFEN
HOHO
RIGHT ON, MAN!
EIN LAHMER HAUFEN, EIN LAHMER HAUFEN!
IHR SEID DOCH NICHTS ALS EIN MÜDER LAHMER HAUFEN!
Jetzt bin ich dran und da komme ich dreist...
was dieser Auftritt mal wieder beweist!
doch wenn du mich bescheißt, dann merk dir eins du Flasche:
Ich bin der Chef mit der Hand in der Tasche
und dem Finger am Abzug
Kommst du mir blöd, mann machst du glllum.
KOF KOF KOF

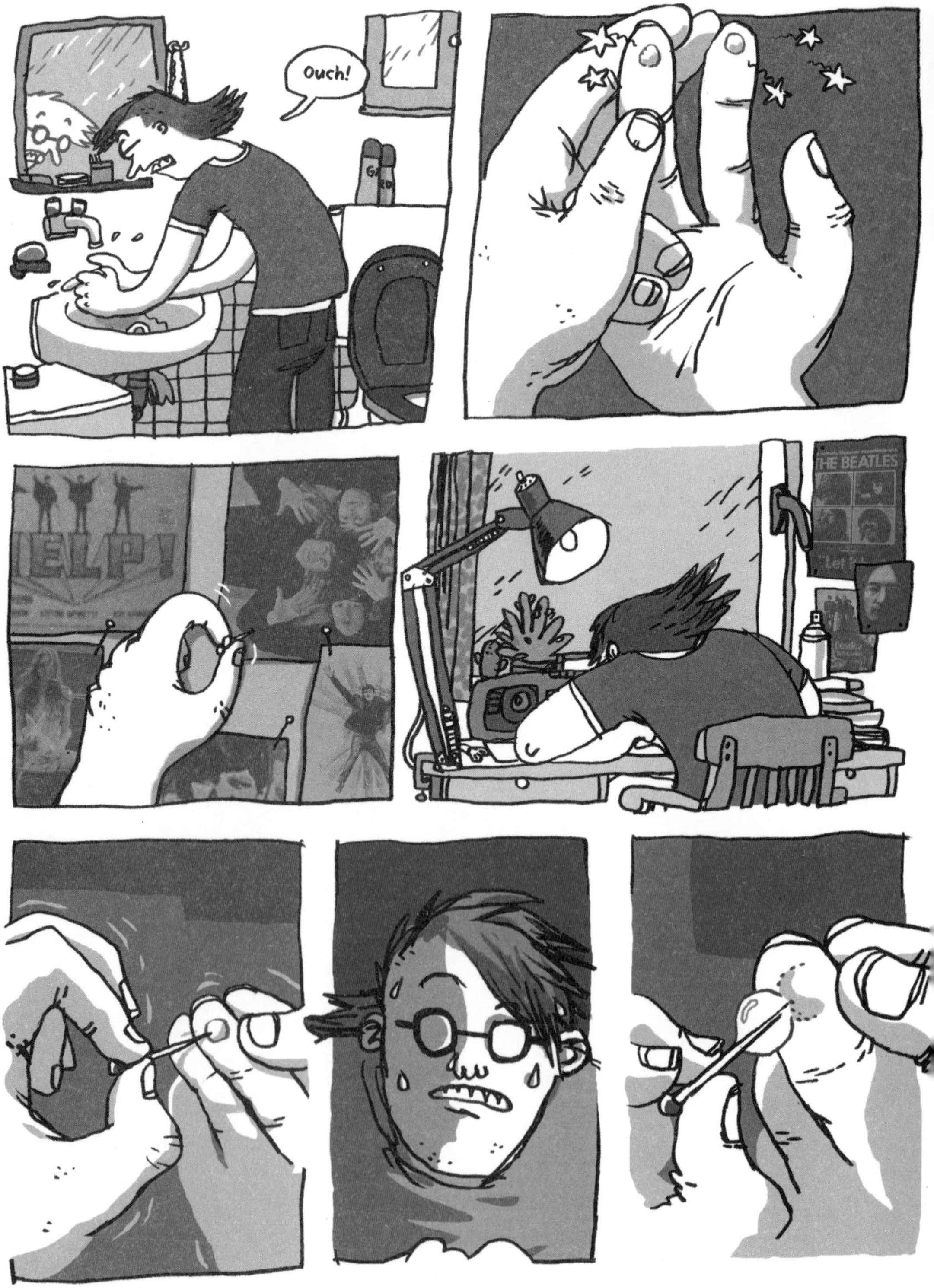
Ouch!
THE BEATLES

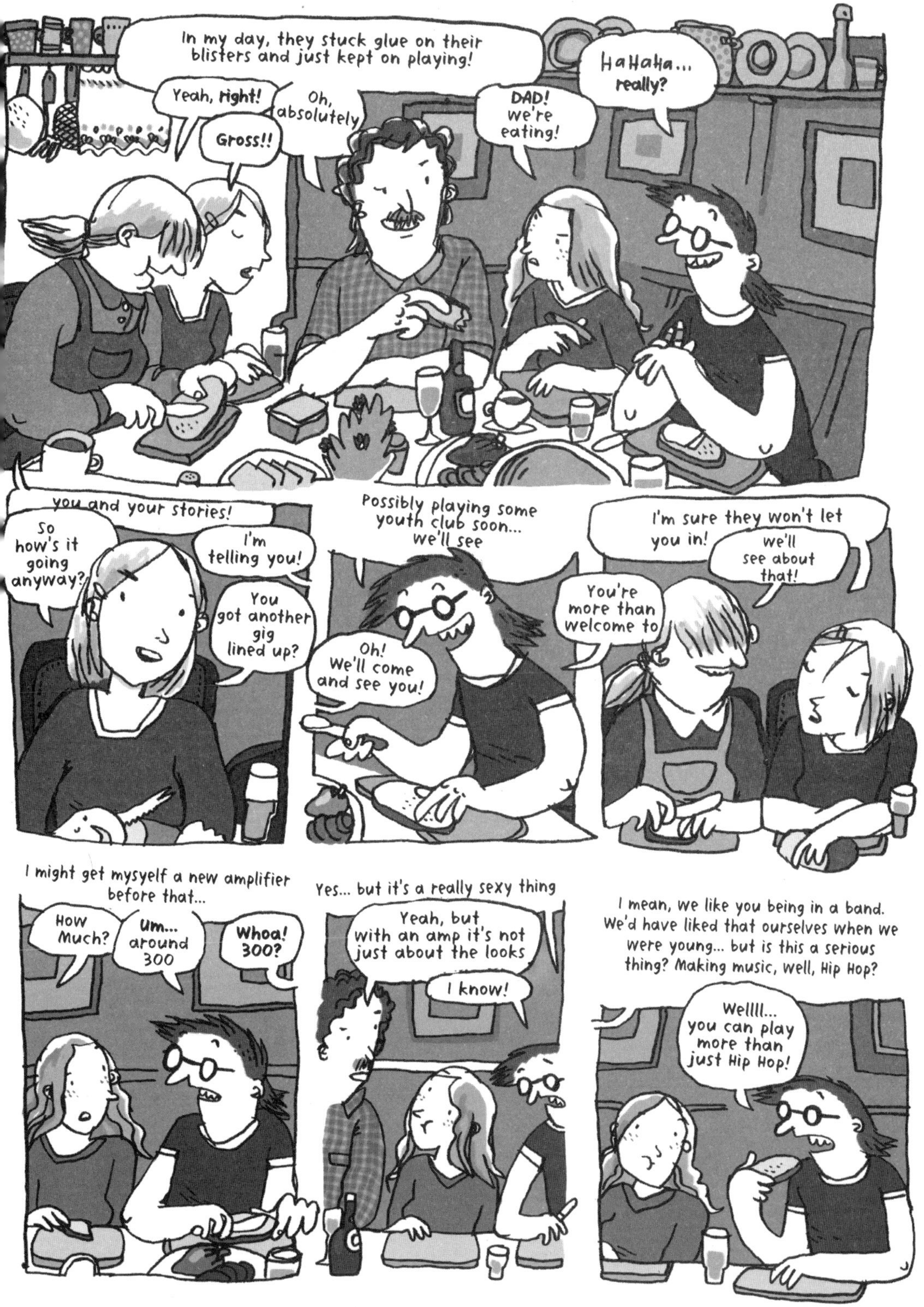
In my day, they stuck glue on their blisters and just kept on playing!
Yeah, right!
Gross!!
Oh, absolutely
DAD! we're eating!
HaHaHa... really?
you and your stories!
So how's it going anyway?
I'm telling you!
You got another gig lined up?
Possibly playing some youth club soon... we'll see
Oh! We'll come and see you!
I'm sure they won't let you in!
we'll see about that!
You're more than welcome to
I might get mysyelf a new amplifier before that...
How Much?
Um... around 300
Whoa! 300?
Yes... but it's a really sexy thing
Yeah, but with an amp it's not just about the looks
I know!
I mean, we like you being in a band. We'd have liked that ourselves when we were young... but is this a serious thing? Making music, well, Hip Hop?
Wellll... you can play more than just Hip Hop!

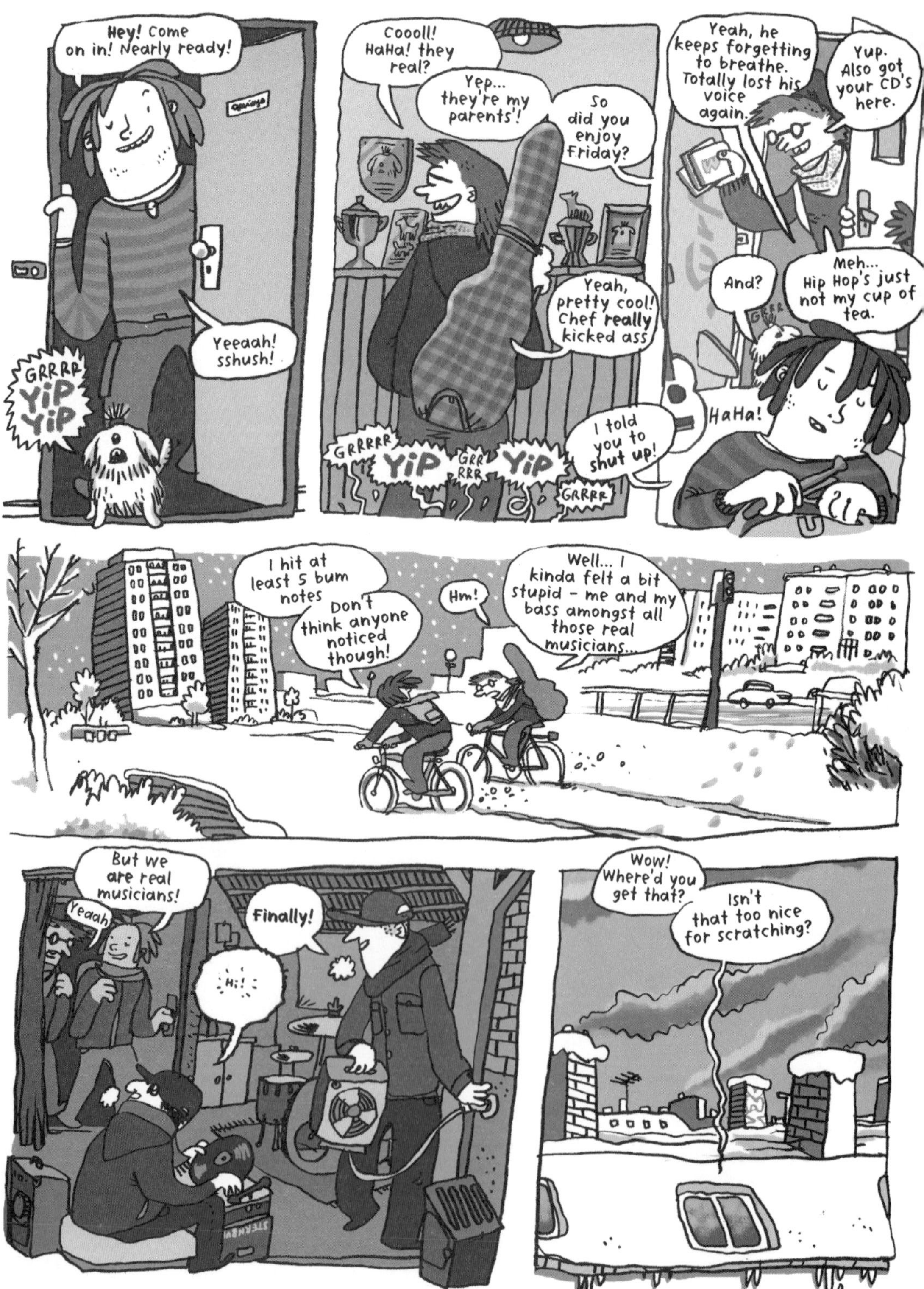
Hey! Come on in! Nearly ready!
Yeeaah! sshush!
GRRRR YIP YIP
Cooool! HaHa! they real?
Yep... they're my parents'!
So did you enjoy Friday?
Yeah, pretty cool! Chef really kicked ass
GRRRRR YIP GRR RRR YIP GRRRR
I told you to shut up!
Yeah, he keeps forgetting to breathe. Totally lost his voice again.
Yup. Also got your CD's here.
And?
Meh... Hip Hop's just not my cup of tea.
GRRR
HaHa!
I hit at least 5 bum notes
Don't think anyone noticed though!
Hm!
Well... I kinda felt a bit stupid - me and my bass amongst all those real musicians...
But we are real musicians!
Yeaah
Finally!
Hi!
Wow! Where'd you get that?
Isn't that too nice for scratching?

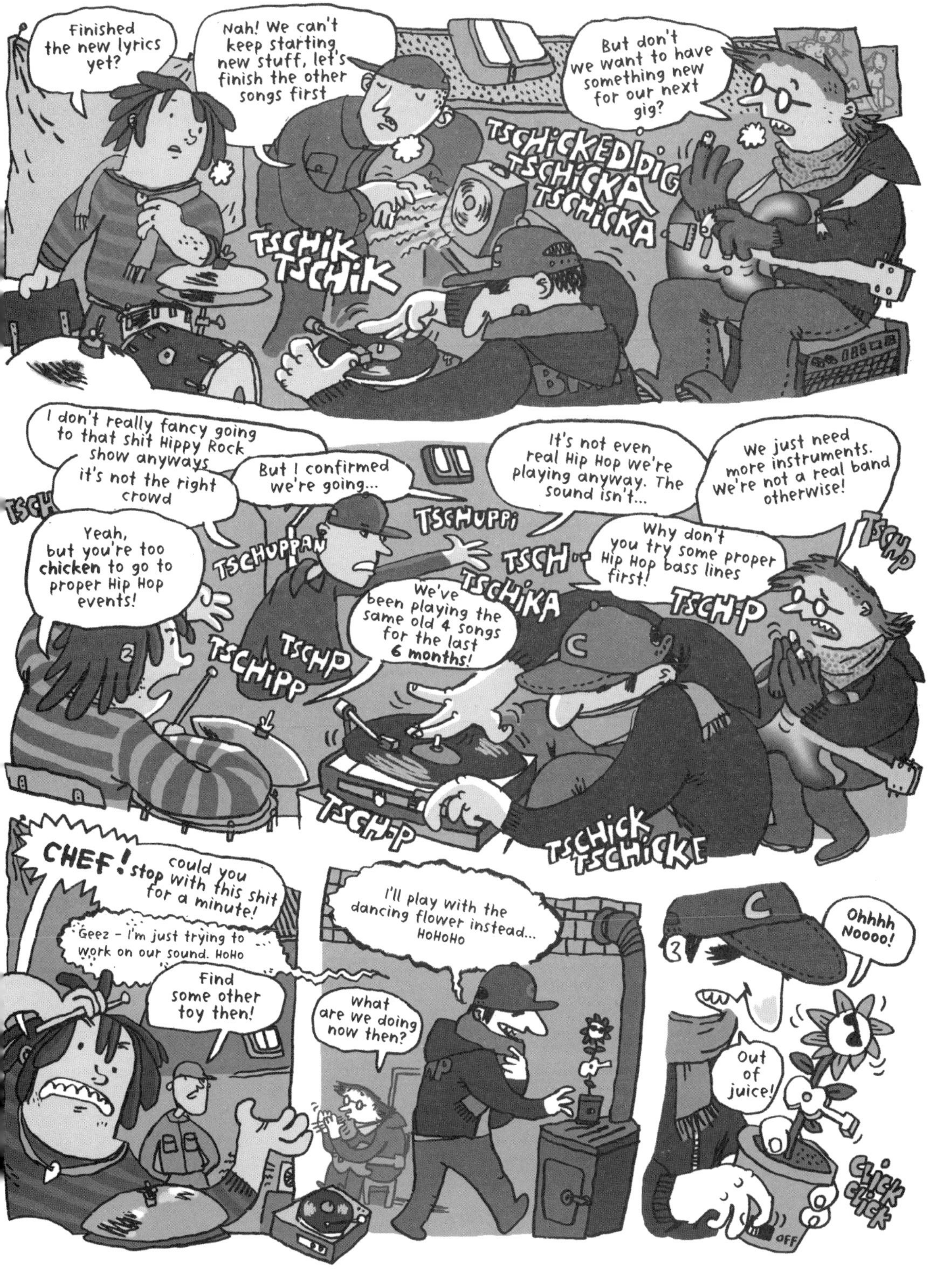
Finished the new lyrics yet?
Nah! We can't keep starting new stuff, let's finish the other songs first
But don't we want to have something new for our next gig?
TSCHICKEDIDIG TSCHICKA TSCHICKA
TSCHIK TSCHIK
I don't really fancy going to that shit Hippy Rock show anyways
it's not the right crowd
But I confirmed we're going...
It's not even real Hip Hop we're playing anyway. The sound isn't...
We just need more instruments. We're not a real band otherwise!
TSCH
Yeah, but you're too **chicken** to go to proper Hip Hop events!
TSCHUPPAN
TSCHUPPI
TSCH-
TSCHIKA
Why don't you try some proper Hip Hop bass lines first!
TSCHP
We've been playing the same old 4 songs for the last **6 months**!
TSCH-P
TSCHP
TSCHIPP
TSCH-P
TSCHICK TSCHICKE
CHEF! could you stop with this shit for a minute!
Geez - I'm just trying to work on our sound. HoHo
Find some other toy then!
I'll play with the dancing flower instead... HOHOHO
What are we doing now then?
Ohhhh Noooo!
Out of juice!
CLICK CLICK
OFF

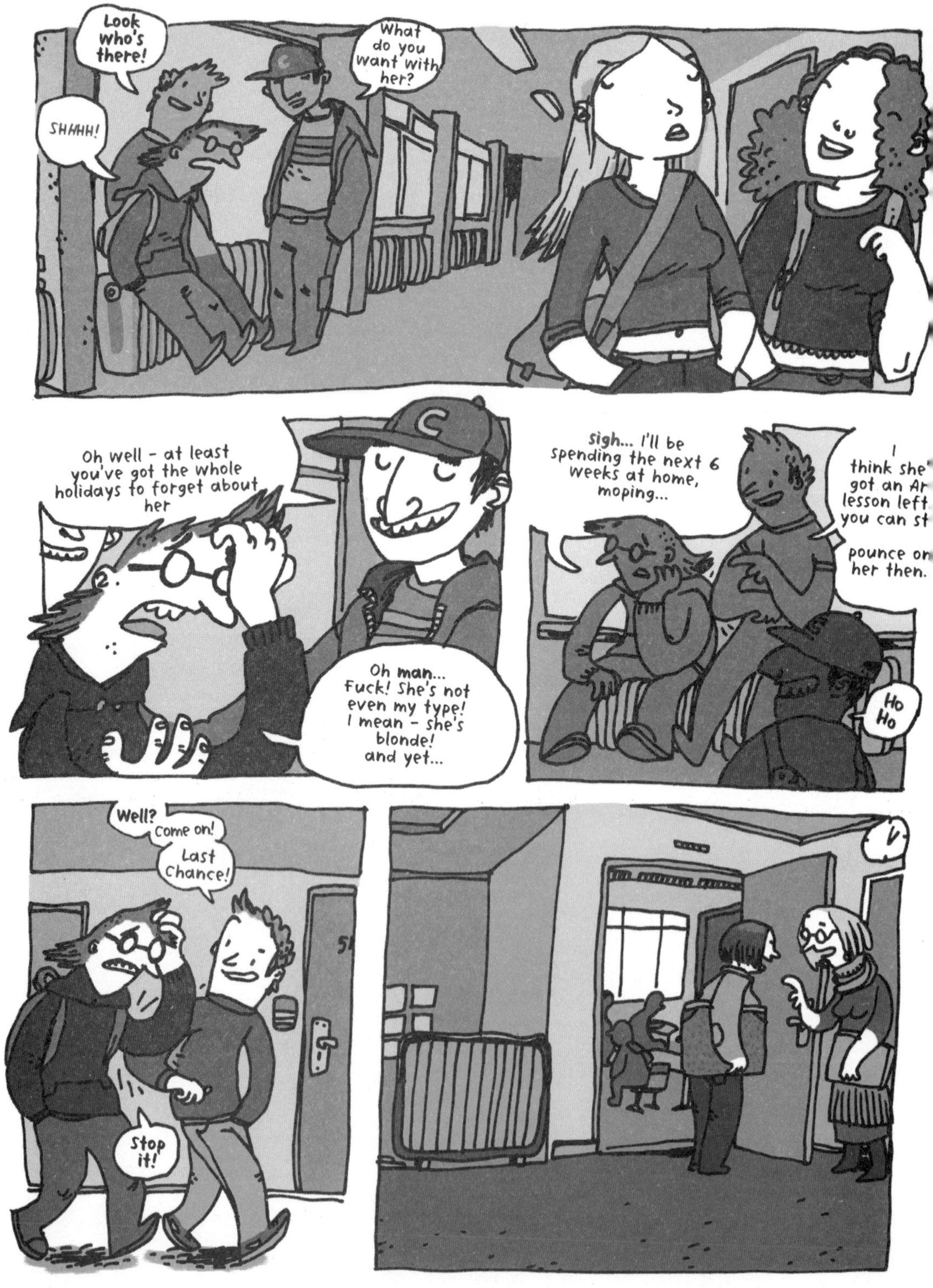

Look who's there!
SHHHH!
What do you want with her?
Oh well - at least you've got the whole holidays to forget about her
Oh man... Fuck! She's not even my type! I mean - she's blonde! and yet...
sigh... I'll be spending the next 6 weeks at home, moping...
I think she' got an Ar lesson left you can st pounce on her then.
Ho Ho
Well?
Come on!
Last Chance!
Stop it!

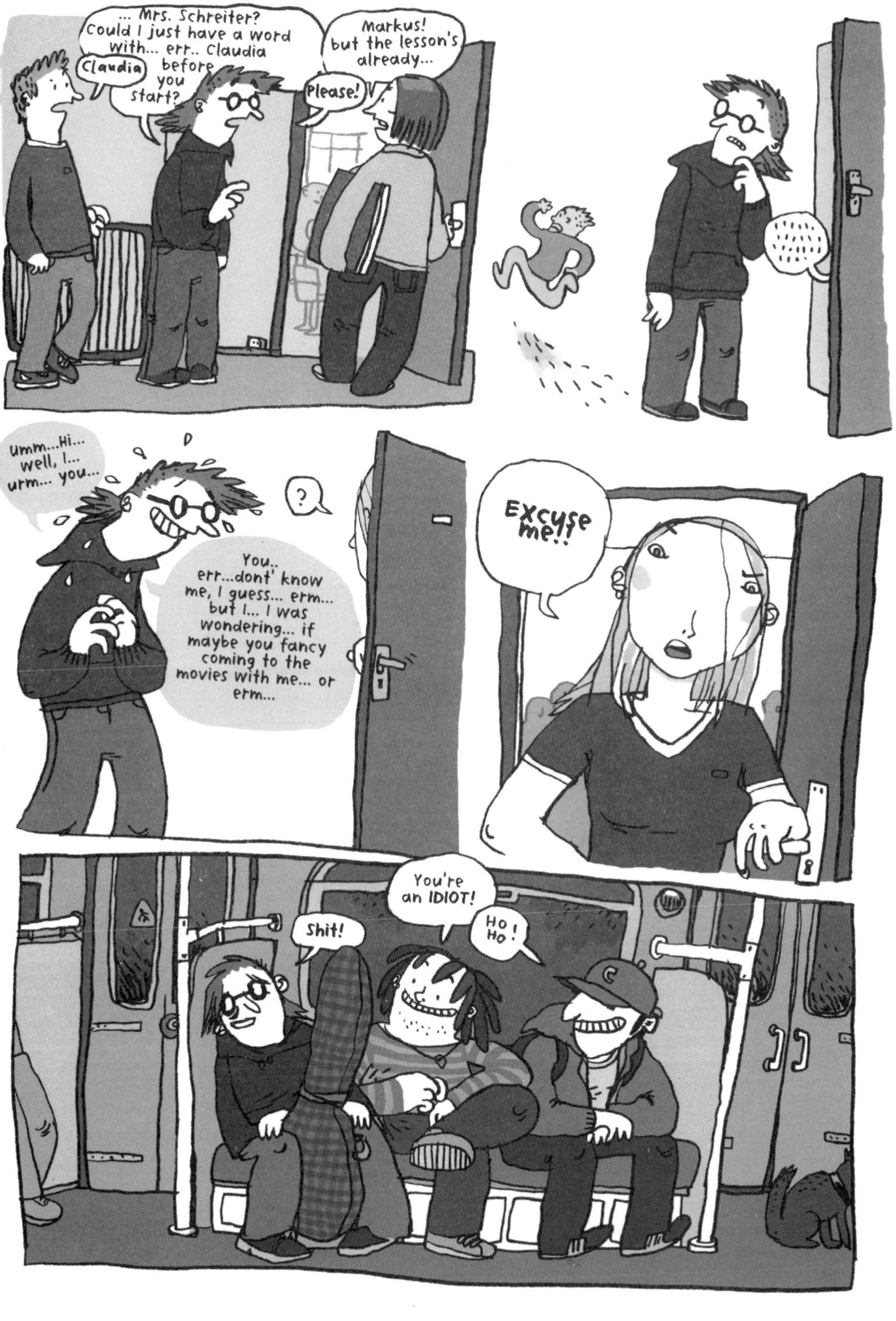
... Mrs. Schreiter? Could I just have a word with... err.. Claudia before you start?
Claudia
Markus! but the lesson's already...
Please!
umm...Hi... well, I... urm... you...
?
You.. err...dont' know me, I guess... erm... but I... I was wondering... if maybe you fancy coming to the movies with me... or erm...
Excuse me!!
You're an IDIOT!
Shit!
Ho! Ho!

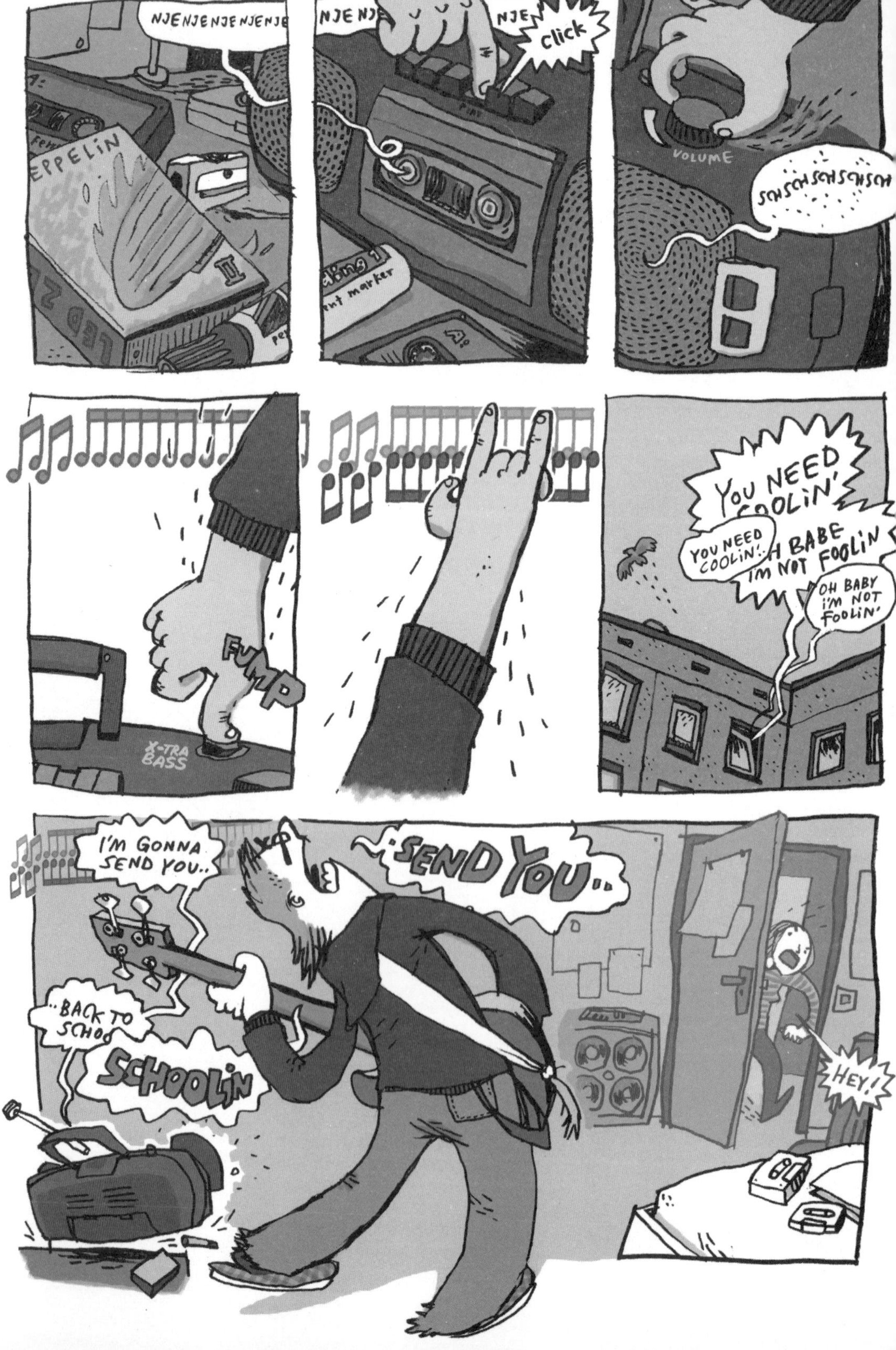
NJENJENJENJENJE
ZEPPELIN
II
NJENJ
NJE
click
ent marker
VOLUME
SCHSCHSCHSCHSCH
FUMP
X-TRA BASS
YOU NEED COOLIN'
YOU NEED COOLIN'..
OH BABE I'M NOT FOOLIN
OH BABY I'M NOT FOOLIN'
I'M GONNA SEND YOU..
SEND YOU..
..BACK TO SCHO
SCHOOLIN
HEY!

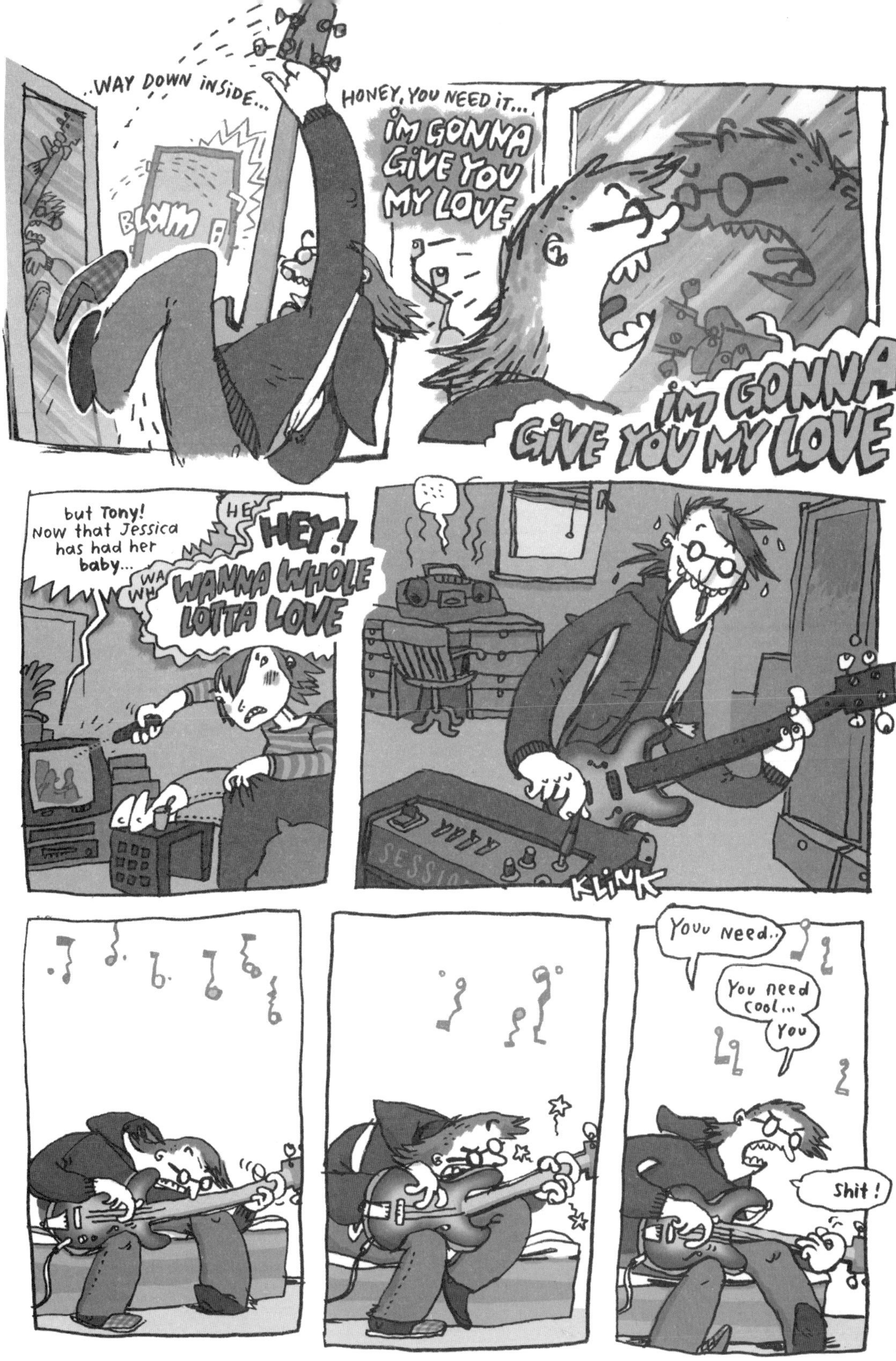
..WAY DOWN INSIDE...
BLAM
HONEY, YOU NEED IT...
IM GONNA GIVE YOU MY LOVE
IM GONNA GIVE YOU MY LOVE
but Tony! Now that Jessica has had her baby...
HEY!
WANNA WHOLE LOTTA LOVE
KLINK
Youu need..
You need cool...
You
Shit!

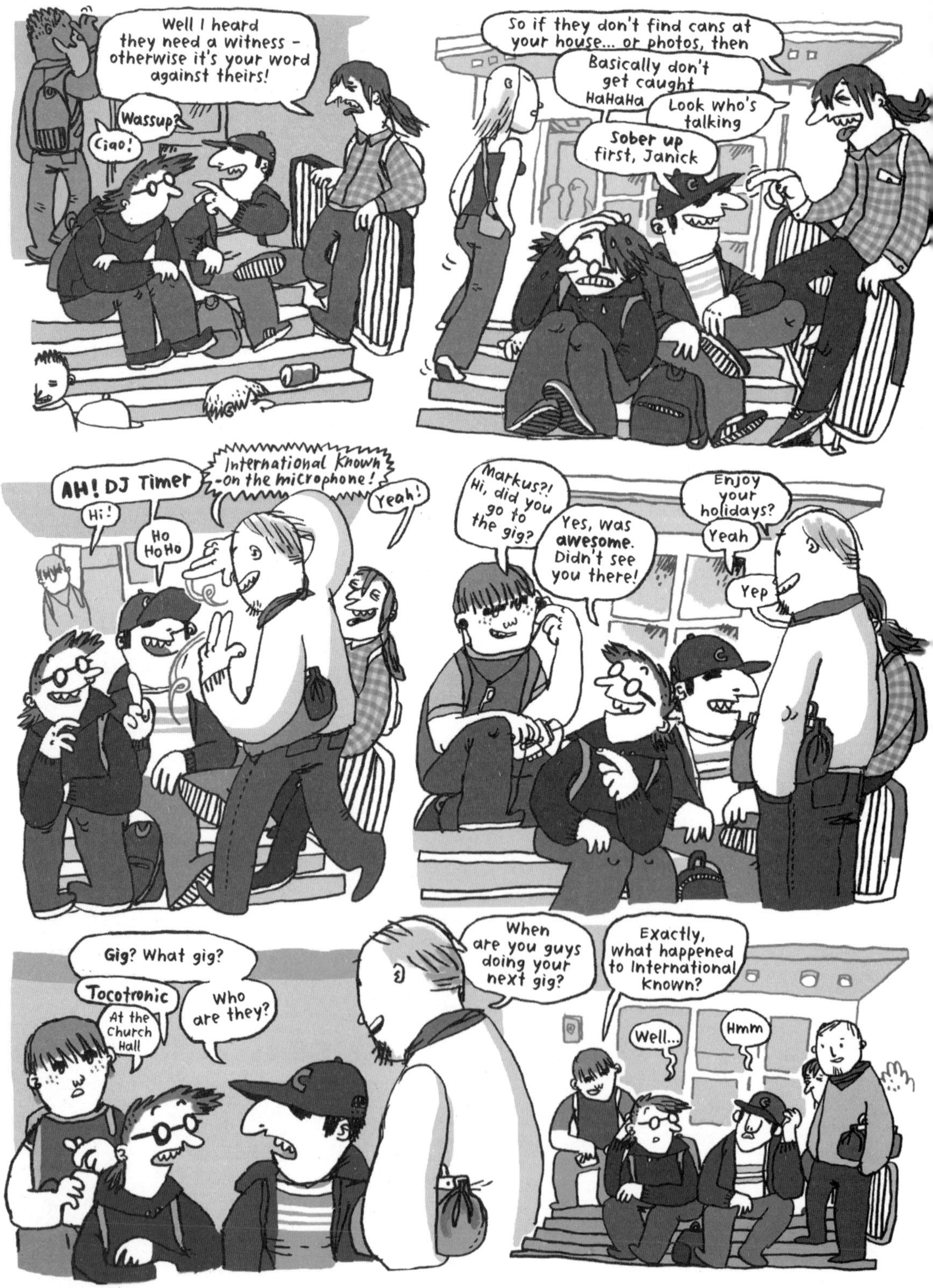
Well I heard they need a witness - otherwise it's your word against theirs!
Wassup?
Ciao!
So if they don't find cans at your house... or photos, then
Basically don't get caught
HaHaHa
Look who's talking
Sober up first, Janick
AH! DJ Timer
Hi!
International Known -on the microphone!
Ho HoHo
Yeah!
Markus?! Hi, did you go to the gig?
Yes, was awesome. Didn't see you there!
Enjoy your holidays?
Yeah
Yep
Gig? What gig?
Tocotronic
At the Church Hall
Who are they?
When are you guys doing your next gig?
Exactly, what happened to International Known?
Well...
Hmm

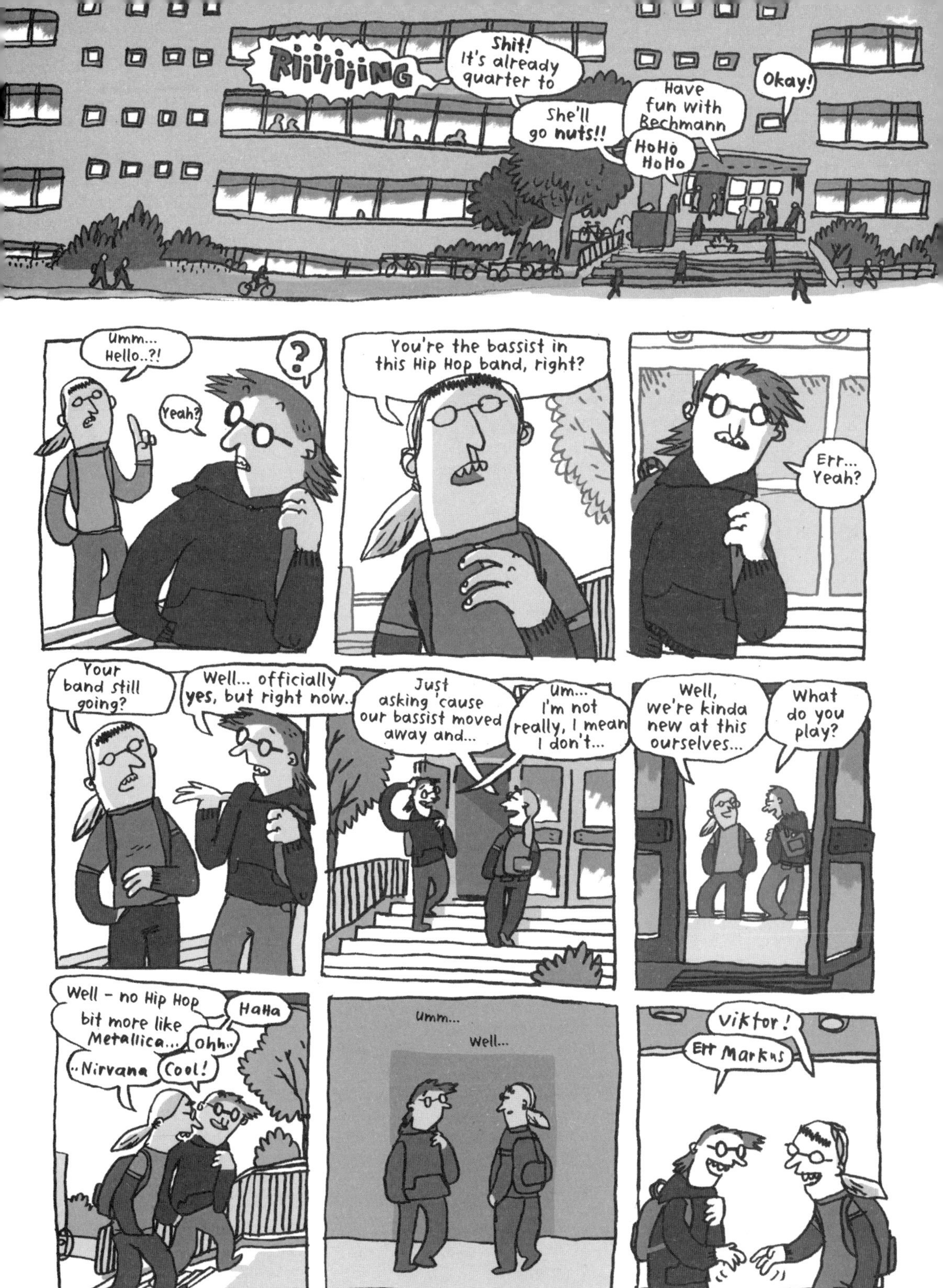
RiiiiiiiNG
Shit! It's already quarter to
She'll go nuts!!
Have fun with Bechmann
HoHo HoHo
Okay!
Umm... Hello..?!
Yeah?
?
You're the bassist in this Hip Hop band, right?
Err... Yeah?
Your band still going?
Well... officially yes, but right now...
Just asking 'cause our bassist moved away and...
Um... I'm not really, I mean I don't...
Well, we're kinda new at this ourselves...
What do you play?
Well - no Hip Hop
bit more like Metallica...
HaHa
Ohh..
..Nirvana
Cool!
Umm...
Well...
Viktor!
Err Markus

(I'D NEVER SEEN VIKTOR BEFORE IN MY LIFE)

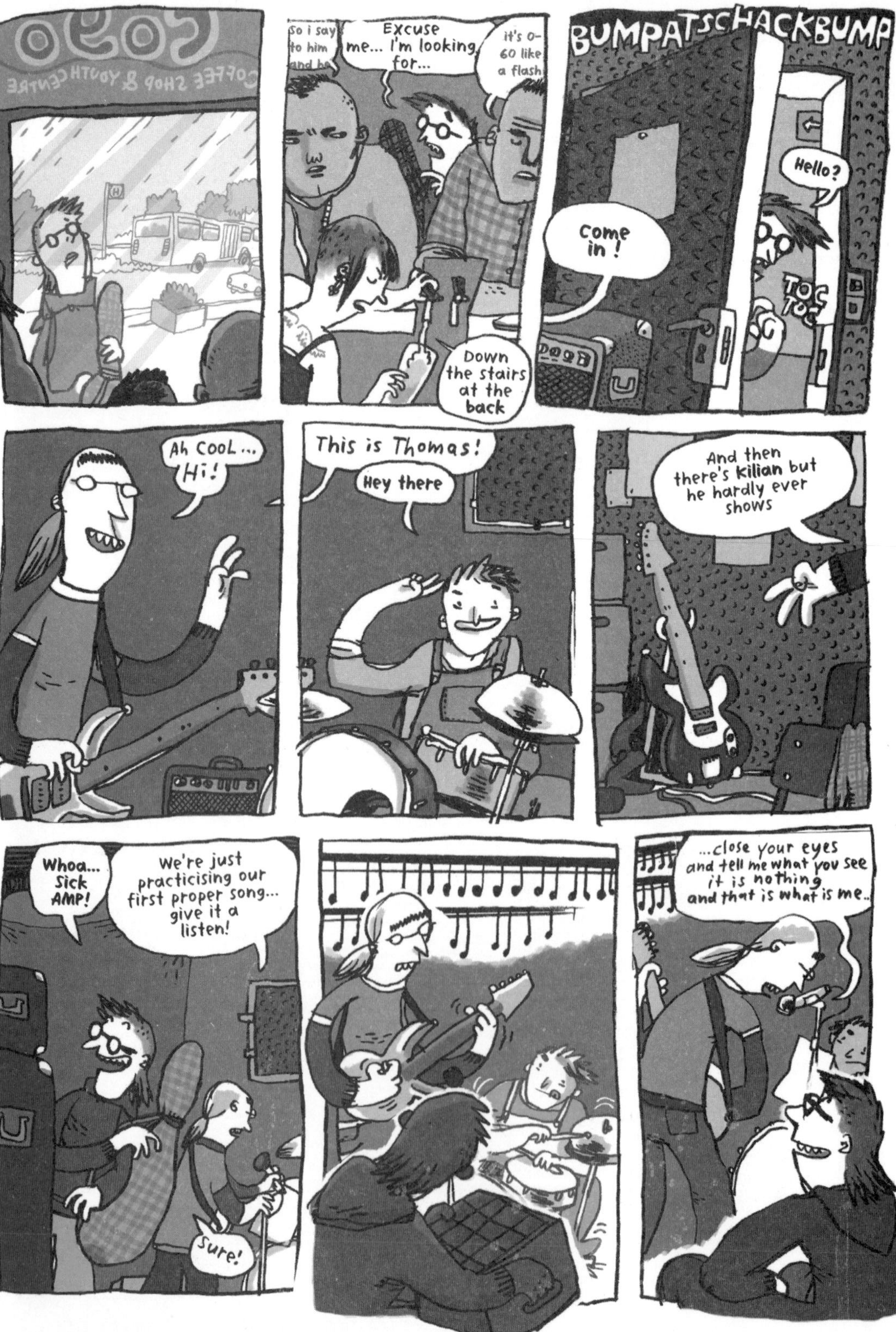

so i say to him
Excuse me... I'm looking for...
it's 0-60 like a flash
Down the stairs at the back
BUMPATSCHACKBUMP
Hello?
TOC TOC
Come in!
Ah COOL... Hi!
This is Thomas!
Hey there
And then there's kilian but he hardly ever shows
Whoa... Sick AMP!
We're just practicising our first proper song... give it a listen!
Sure!
...close your eyes and tell me what you see it is nothing and that is what is me..

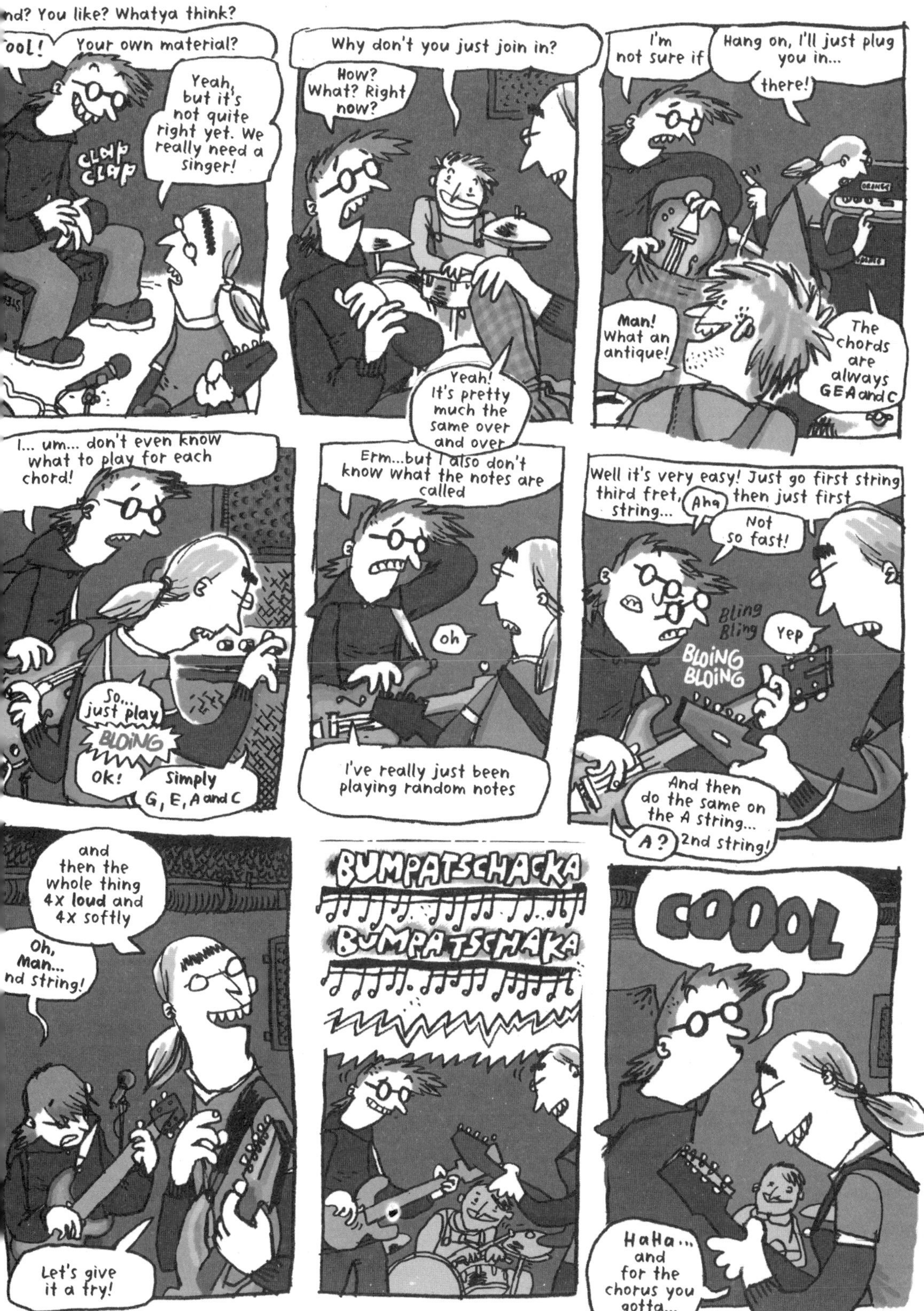

nd? You like? Whatya think?
ooL!
Your own material?
Yeah, but it's not quite right yet. We really need a singer!
CLAP CLAP
Why don't you just join in?
How? What? Right now?
Yeah! It's pretty much the same over and over
I'm not sure if
Hang on, I'll just plug you in...
there!
Man! What an antique!
The chords are always GEA and C
I... um... don't even know what to play for each chord!
So... just play
BLOING
Ok!
Simply G, E, A and C
Erm...but I also don't know what the notes are called
oh
I've really just been playing random notes
Well it's very easy! Just go first string third fret,
Aha
then just first string...
Not so fast!
Bling Bling
Yep
BLOING BLOING
And then do the same on the A string...
A?
2nd string!
and then the whole thing 4x loud and 4x softly
Oh, Man... nd string!
Let's give it a try!
BUMPATSCHACKA
BUMPATSCHAKA
COOOL
HaHa... and for the chorus you gotta...

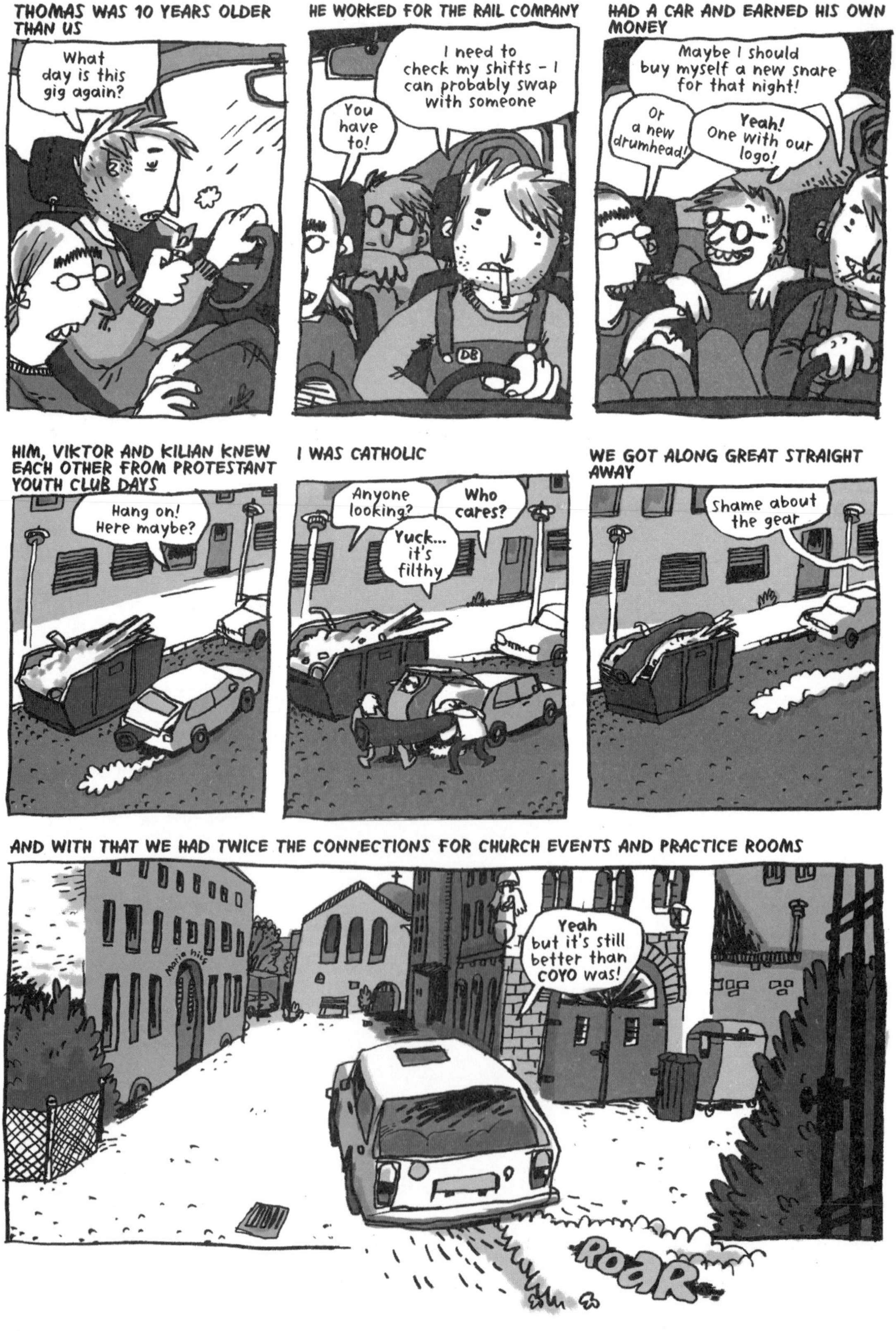
THOMAS WAS 10 YEARS OLDER THAN US
What day is this gig again?
HE WORKED FOR THE RAIL COMPANY
I need to check my shifts - I can probably swap with someone
You have to!
DB
HAD A CAR AND EARNED HIS OWN MONEY
Maybe I should buy myself a new snare for that night!
Or a new drumhead!
Yeah! One with our logo!
HIM, VIKTOR AND KILIAN KNEW EACH OTHER FROM PROTESTANT YOUTH CLUB DAYS
Hang on! Here maybe?
I WAS CATHOLIC
Anyone looking?
Who cares?
Yuck... it's filthy
WE GOT ALONG GREAT STRAIGHT AWAY
Shame about the gear
AND WITH THAT WE HAD TWICE THE CONNECTIONS FOR CHURCH EVENTS AND PRACTICE ROOMS
Maria hilf
Yeah but it's still better than COYO was!
ROAR

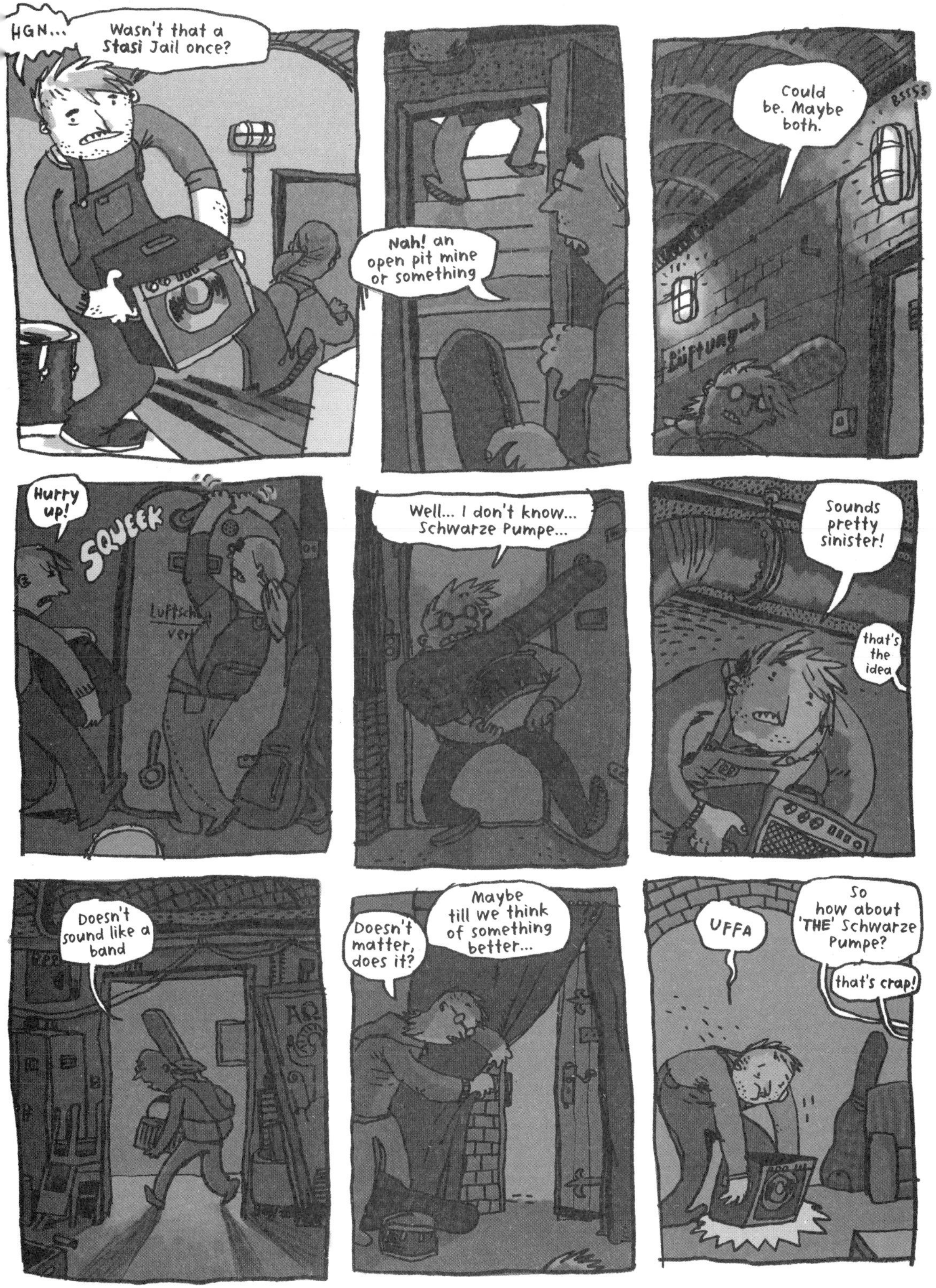
HGN...
Wasn't that a Stasi Jail once?
Nah! an open pit mine or something
Could be. Maybe both.
BSSSS
Lüftung
Hurry up!
SQUEEK
Well... I don't know... Schwarze Pumpe...
Sounds pretty sinister!
that's the idea
Doesn't sound like a band
Doesn't matter, does it?
Maybe till we think of something better...
UFFA
So how about 'THE' Schwarze Pumpe?
that's crap!

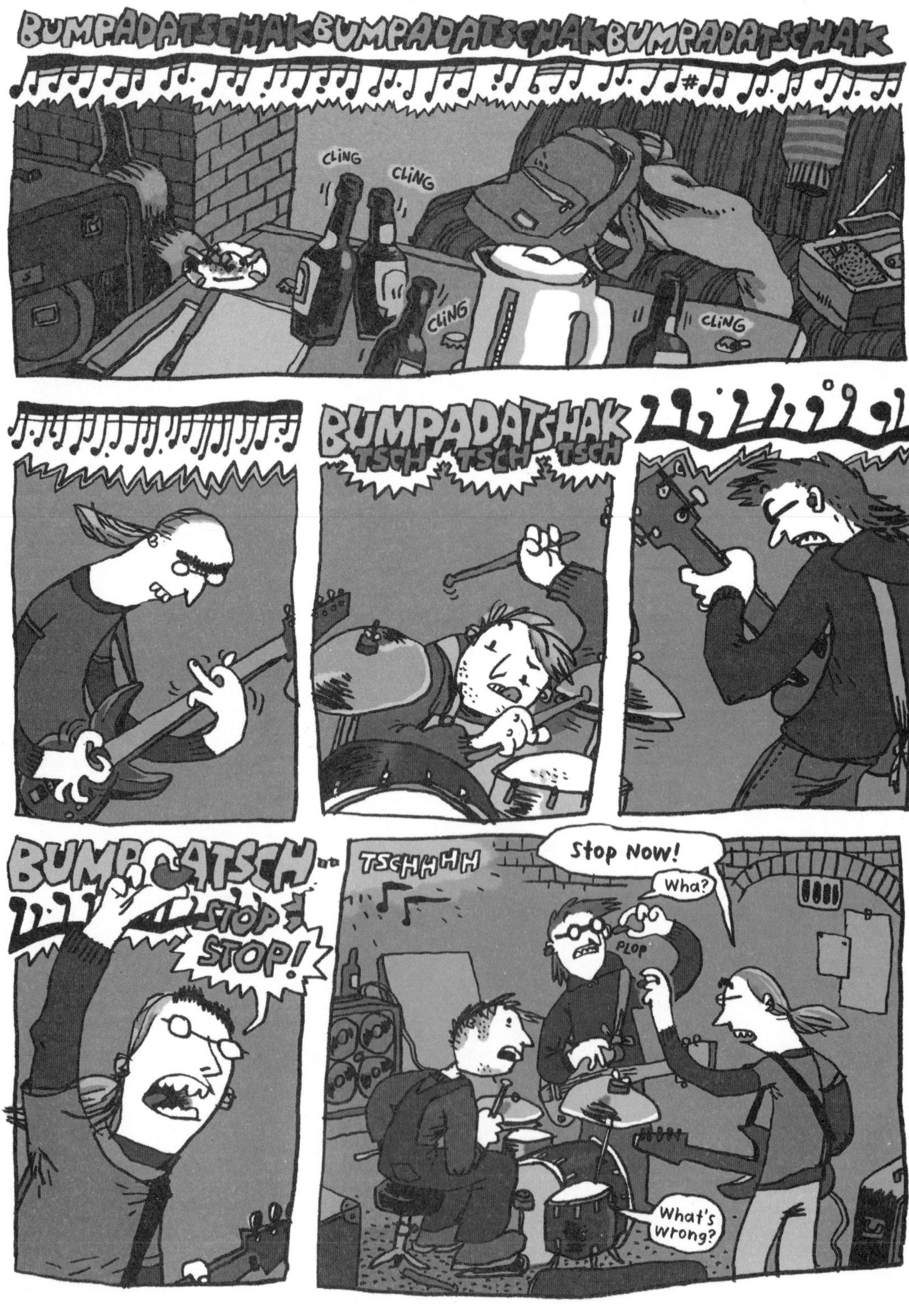

BUMPADATSCHAKBUMPADATSCHAKBUMPADATSCHAK
CLING
CLING
CLING
CLING
BUMPADATSHAK
TSCH TSCH TSCH
BUMPCATSCH
STOP STOP!
TSCHHHHH
Stop Now!
Wha?
PLOP
What's wrong?

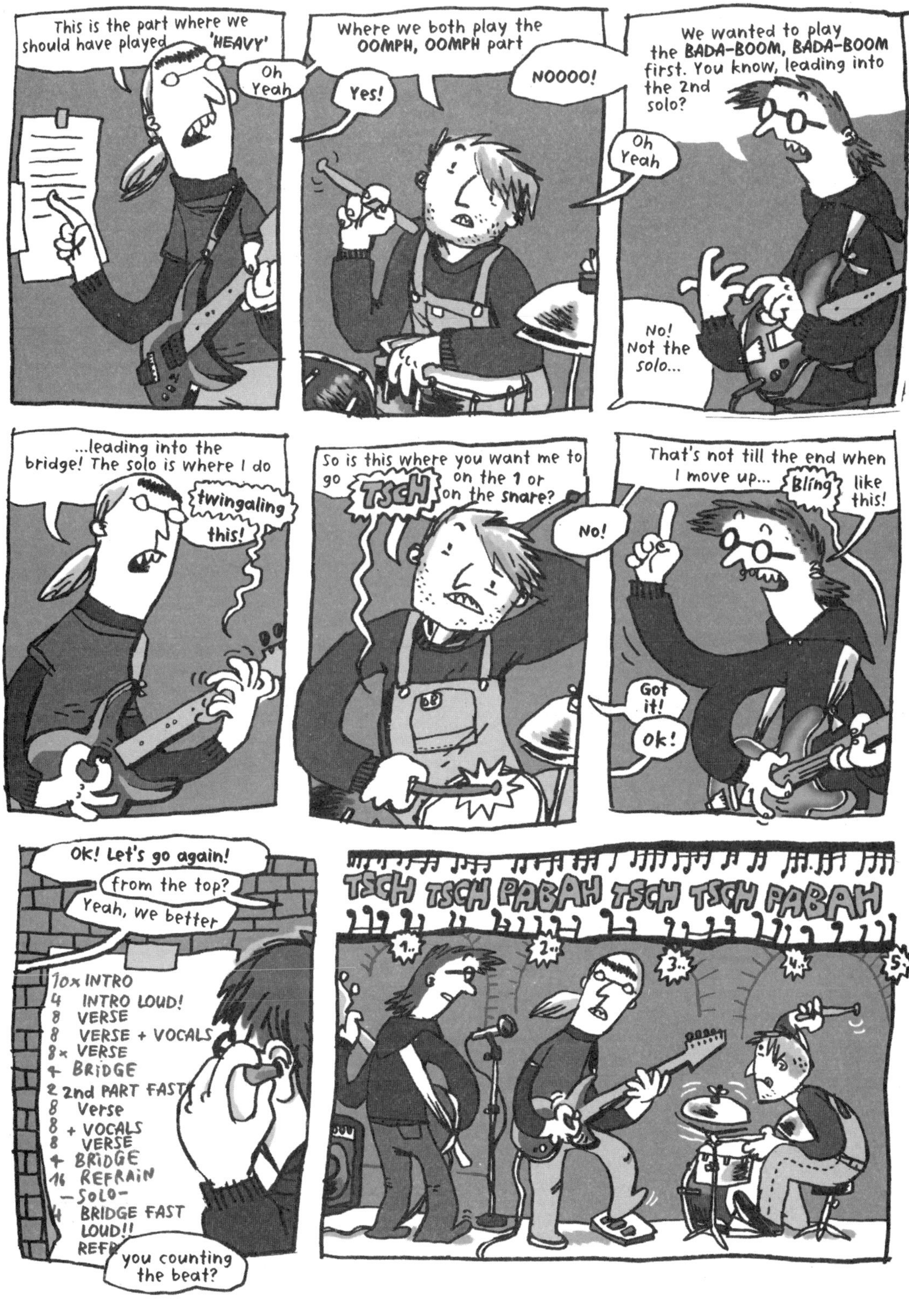

This is the part where we should have played 'HEAVY'
Oh Yeah
Where we both play the OOMPH, OOMPH part
Yes!
NOOOO!
We wanted to play the BADA-BOOM, BADA-BOOM first. You know, leading into the 2nd solo?
Oh Yeah
No! Not the solo...
...leading into the bridge! The solo is where I do
twingaling this!
So is this where you want me to go TSCH on the 1 or on the snare?
No!
That's not till the end when I move up... Bling like this!
Got it!
ok!
Ok! Let's go again!
from the top?
Yeah, we better
10x INTRO
4 INTRO LOUD!
8 VERSE
8 VERSE + VOCALS
8x VERSE
4 BRIDGE
2 2nd PART FAST
8 Verse
8 + VOCALS VERSE
4 BRIDGE
16 REFRAIN
—SOLO—
4 BRIDGE FAST LOUD!!
you counting the beat?
TSCH TSCH PABAH TSCH TSCH PABAH
1..
2..
3..
4..
5..

ONLY 6 MONTHS LATER WE HAD OUR FIRST PERFORMANCE

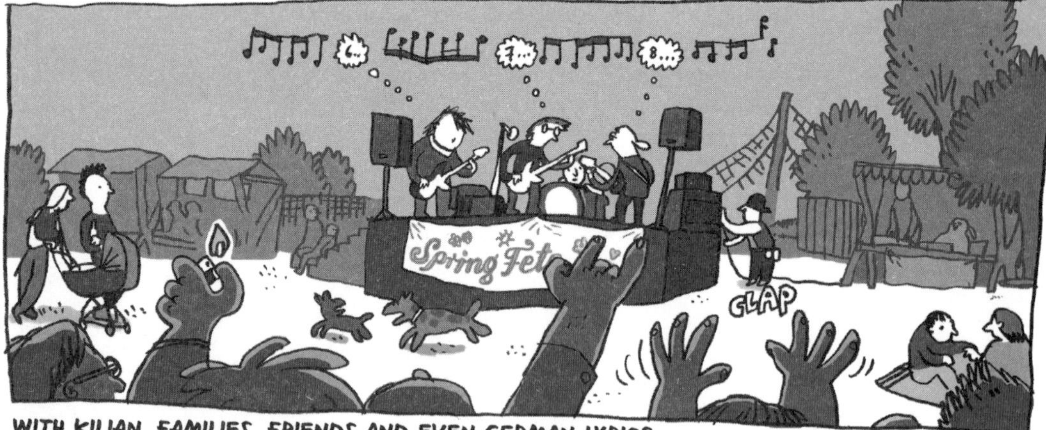
6...
7...
8...
Spring Fet
CLAP

WITH KILIAN, FAMILIES, FRIENDS AND EVEN GERMAN LYRICS

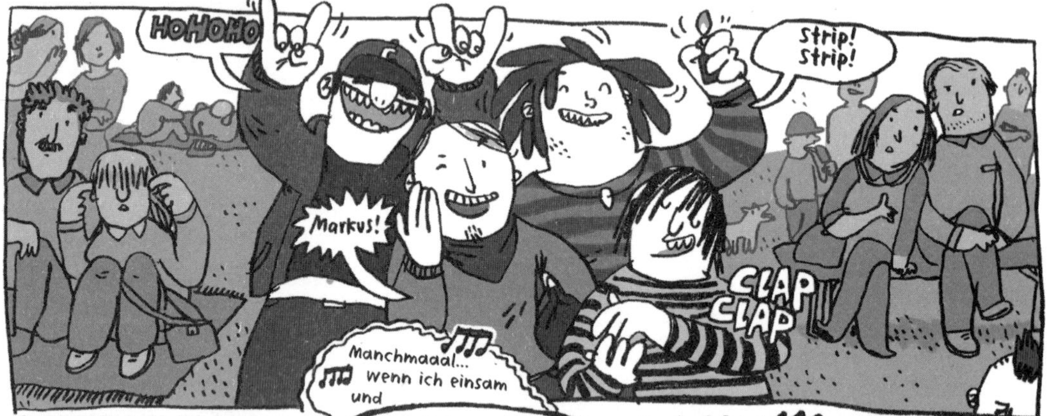
HOHOHO
strip! strip!
Markus!
CLAP CLAP
Manchmaaal... wenn ich einsam und

3 GUESSES AS TO WHO THE NEW SINGER WAS

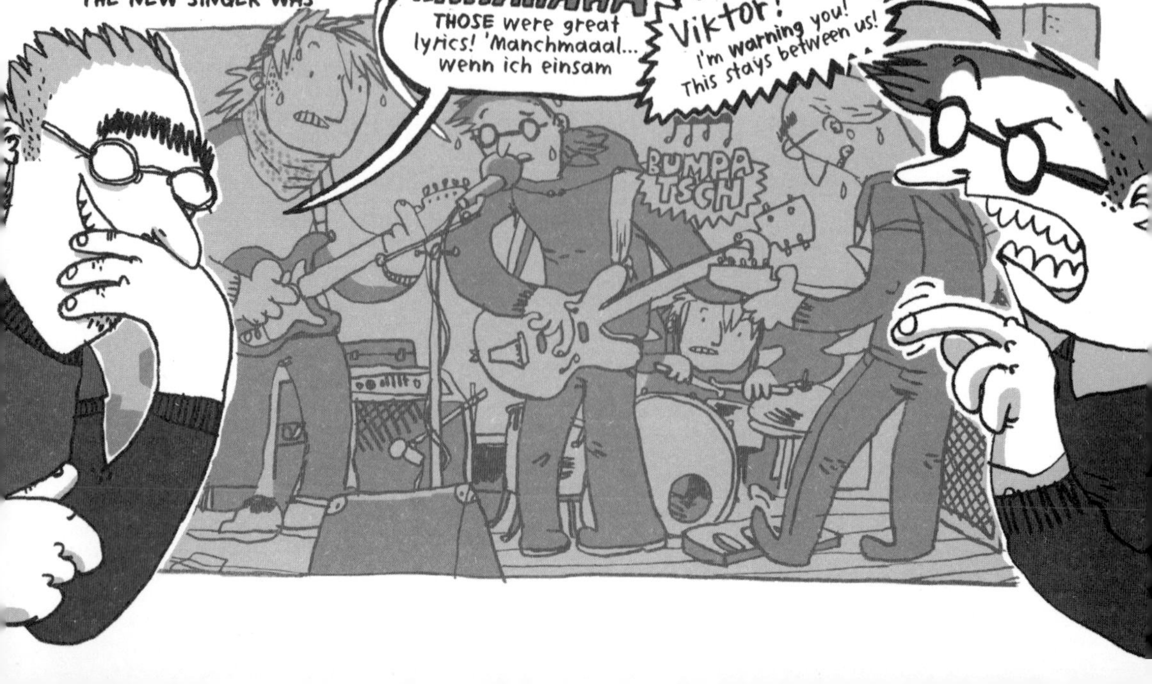
HAHAHAHA THOSE were great lyrics! 'Manchmaaal... wenn ich einsam
Viktor! I'm warning you! This stays between us!
BUMPA TSCH

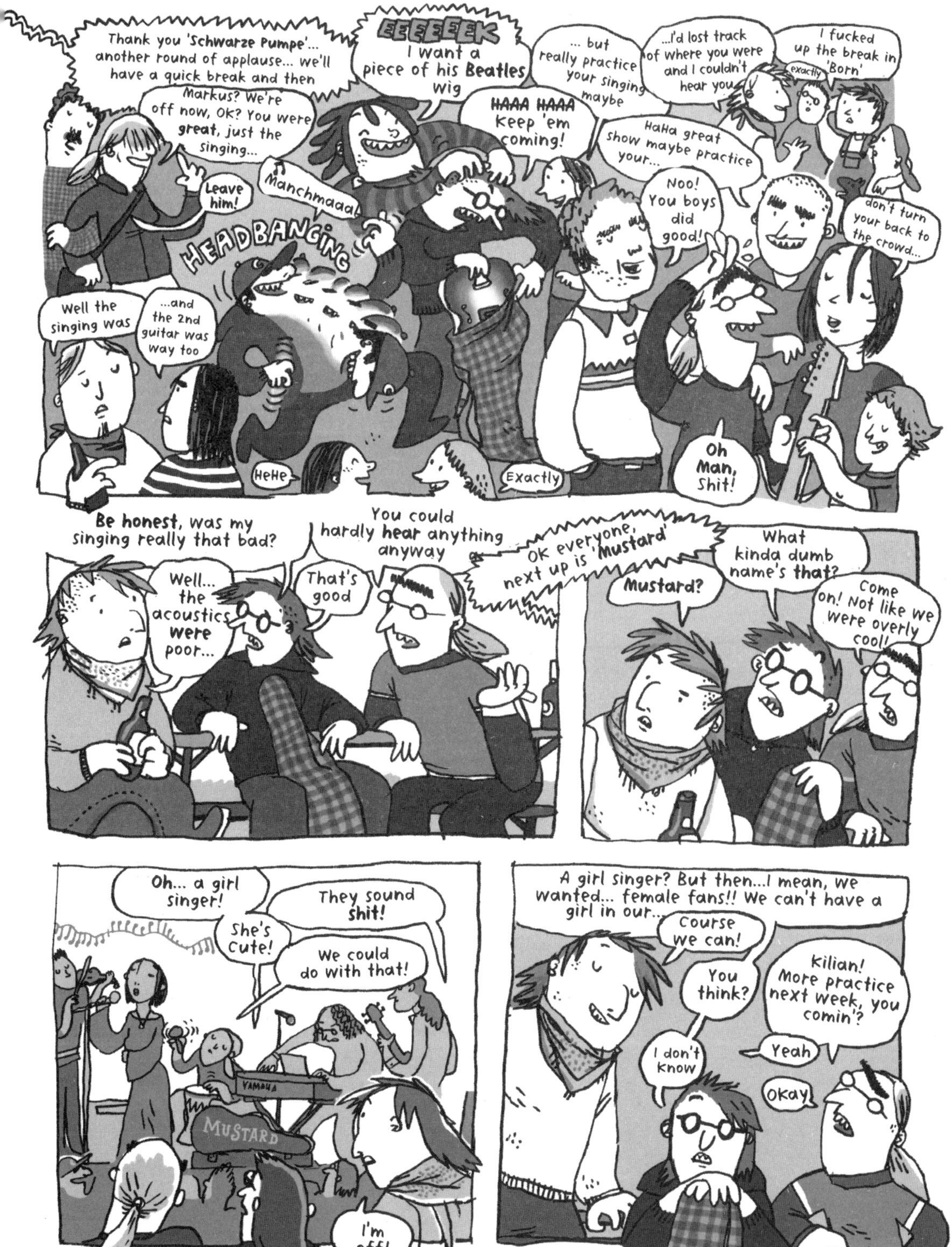
Thank you 'Schwarze Pumpe'... another round of applause... we'll have a quick break and then
EEEEEEK
I want a piece of his Beatles wig
... but really practice your singing maybe
...I'd lost track of where you were and I couldn't hear you
I fucked up the break in 'Born'
exactly
Markus? We're off now, OK? You were great, just the singing...
HAAA HAAA Keep 'em coming!
HaHa great show maybe practice your...
Leave him!
Manchmaaal
Noo! You boys did good!
don't turn your back to the crowd...
HEADBANGING
Well the singing was
...and the 2nd guitar was way too
HeHe
Exactly
Oh Man, Shit!
Be honest, was my singing really that bad?
You could hardly hear anything anyway
Well... the acoustics were poor...
That's good
OK everyone, next up is 'Mustard'
Mustard?
What kinda dumb name's that?
Come on! Not like we were overly cool!
Oh... a girl singer!
They sound shit!
She's cute!
We could do with that!
YAMAHA
MUSTARD
I'm off!
A girl singer? But then...I mean, we wanted... female fans!! We can't have a girl in our...
Course we can!
You think?
Kilian! More practice next week, you comin'?
I don't know
Yeah
Okay

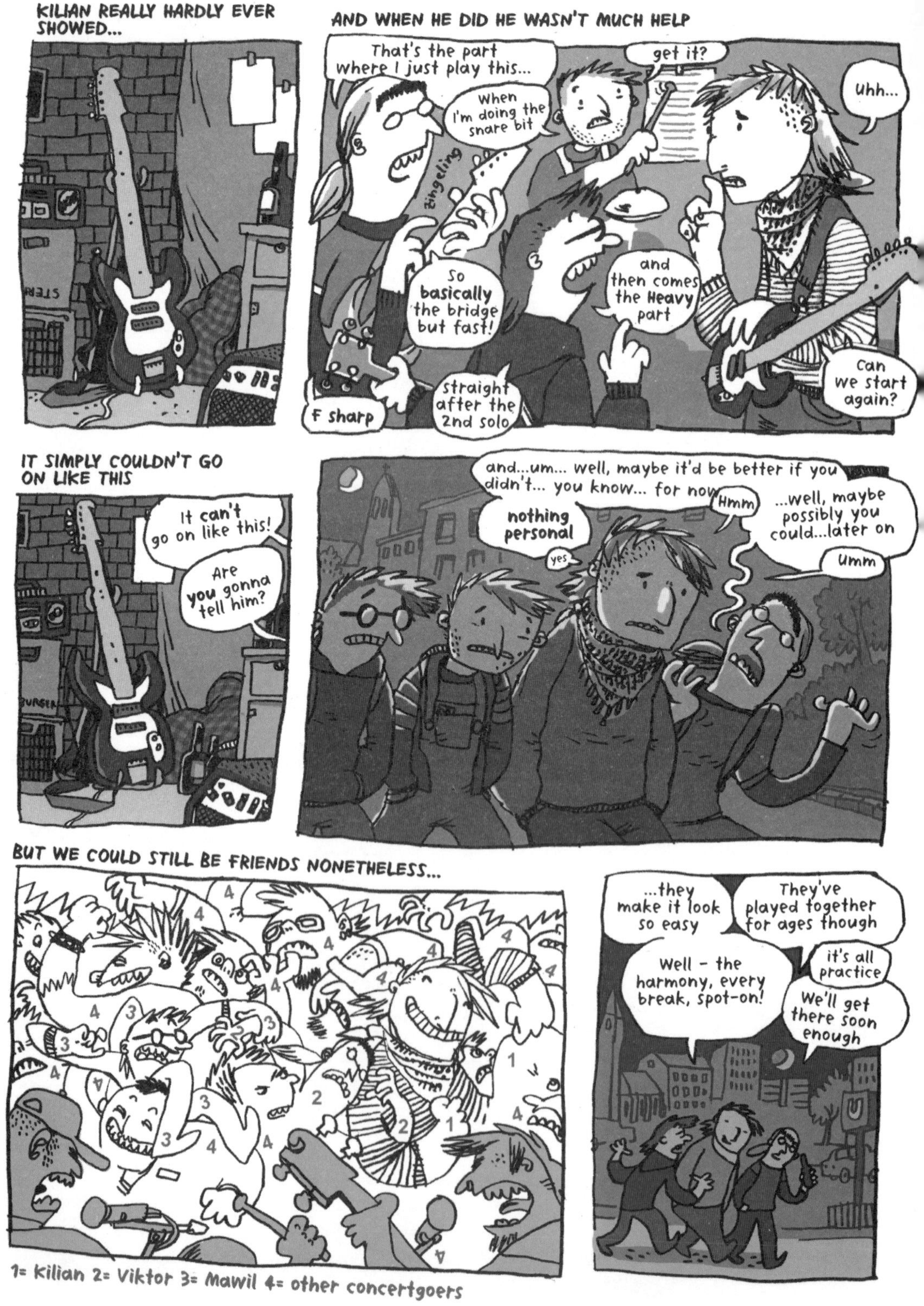
KILIAN REALLY HARDLY EVER SHOWED...
AND WHEN HE DID HE WASN'T MUCH HELP
That's the part where I just play this...
When I'm doing the snare bit
get it?
Uhh...
zingeling
So basically the bridge but fast!
and then comes the Heavy part
F sharp
straight after the 2nd solo
Can we start again?
IT SIMPLY COULDN'T GO ON LIKE THIS
It can't go on like this!
Are you gonna tell him?
and...um... well, maybe it'd be better if you didn't... you know... for now
nothing personal
yes
Hmm
...well, maybe possibly you could...later on
Umm
BUT WE COULD STILL BE FRIENDS NONETHELESS...
...they make it look so easy
They've played together for ages though
Well - the harmony, every break, spot-on!
it's all practice
We'll get there soon enough
1= Kilian 2= Viktor 3= Mawil 4= other concertgoers

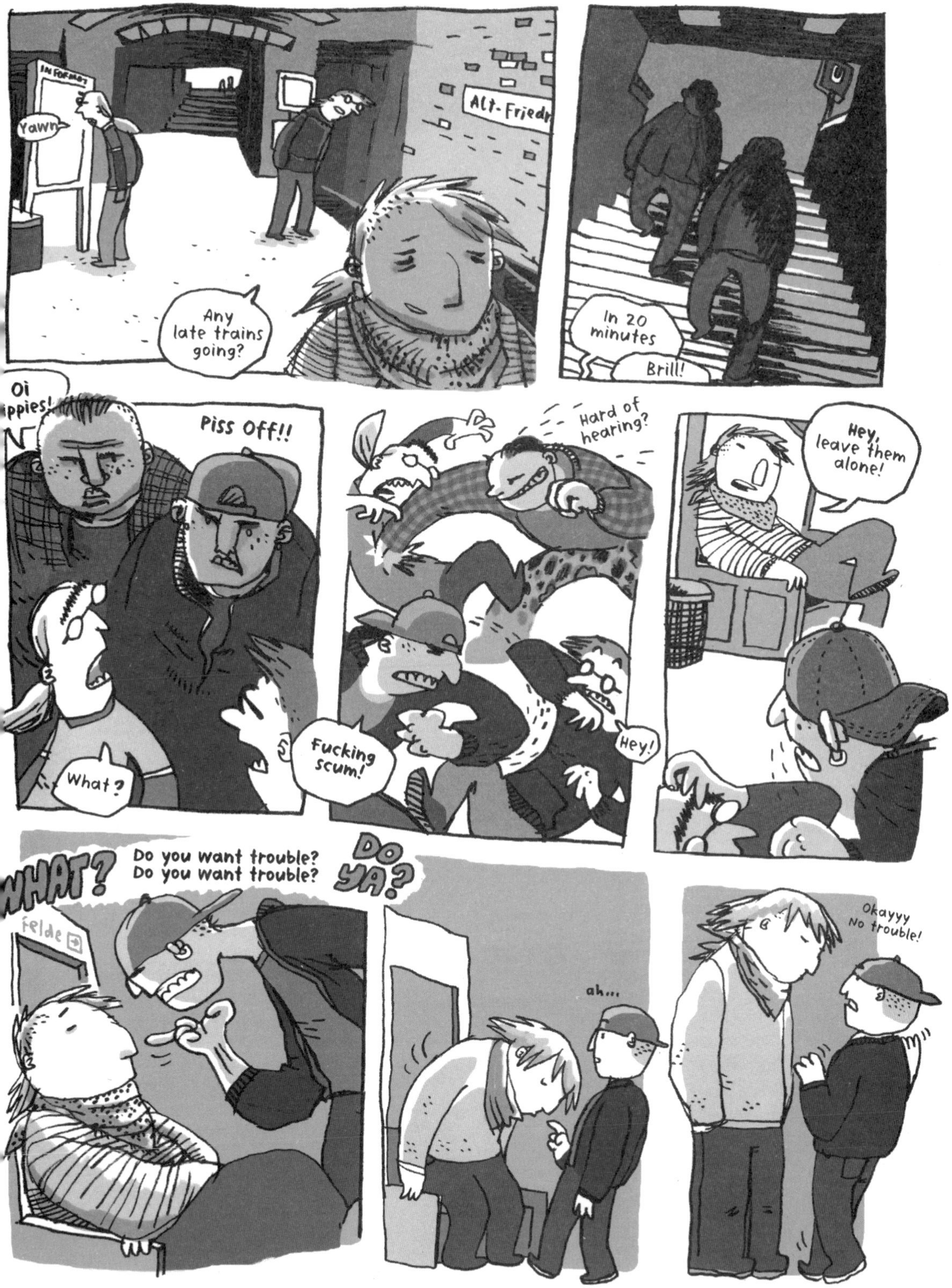
INFORMAT
Yawn
Alt-Friedr
Any late trains going?
In 20 minutes
Brill!
Oi ippies!
Piss Off!!
What?
Hard of hearing?
Fucking scum!
Hey!
Hey, leave them alone!
WHAT?
Do you want trouble? Do you want trouble?
DO YA?
felde
ah...
Okayyy No trouble!

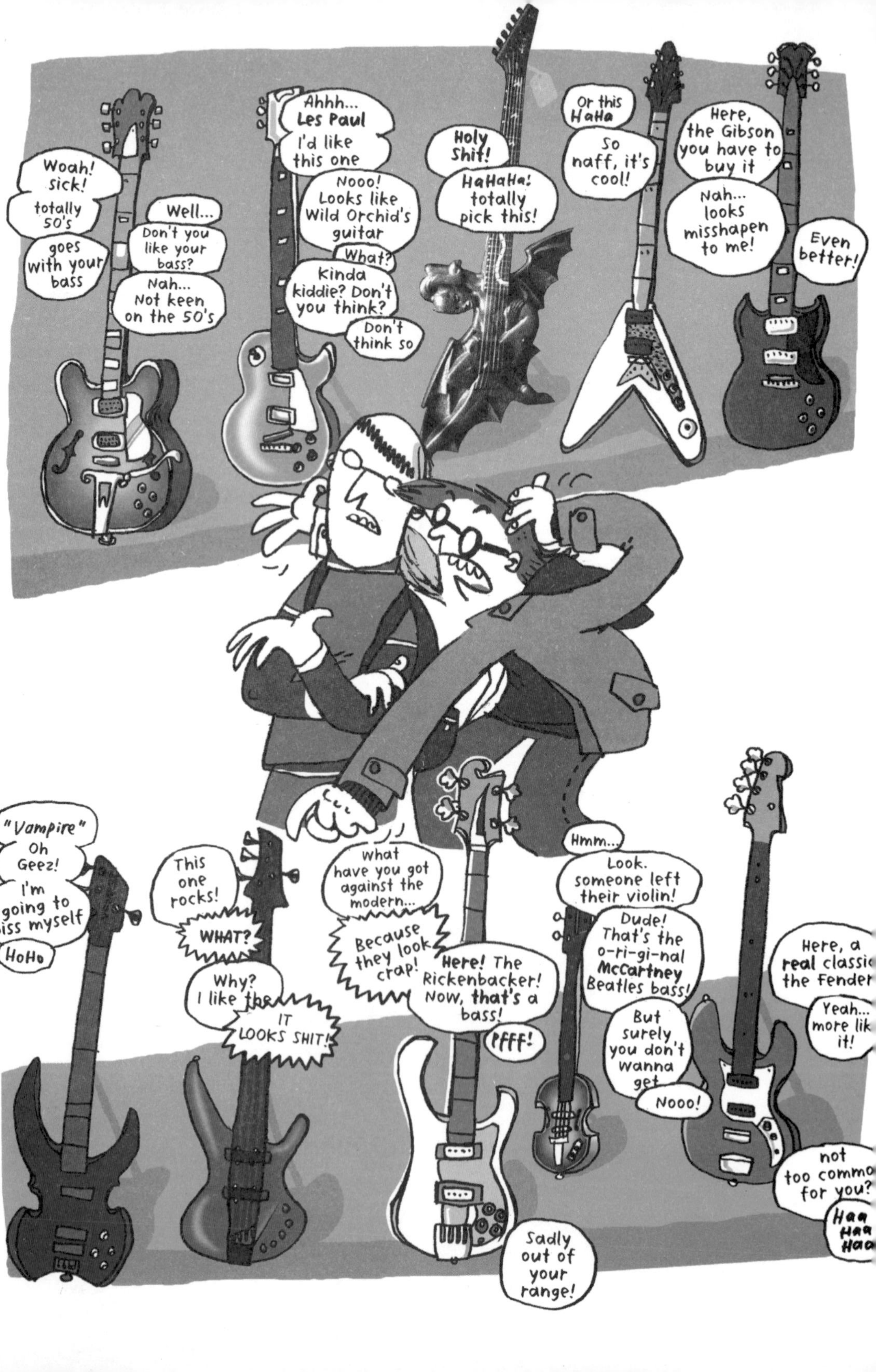

Woah! sick!
totally 50's
goes with your bass
Well...
Don't you like your bass?
Nah... Not keen on the 50's
Ahhh... **Les Paul**
I'd like this one
Nooo! Looks like Wild Orchid's guitar
What?
Kinda kiddie? Don't you think?
Don't think so
Holy Shit!
HaHaHa! totally pick this!
Or this HaHa
So naff, it's cool!
Here, the Gibson you have to buy it
Nah... looks misshapen to me!
Even better!
"Vampire"
Oh Geez!
I'm going to piss myself
HoHo
This one rocks!
WHAT?
Why? I like the
IT LOOKS SHIT!
what have you got against the modern...
Because they look crap!
Here! The Rickenbacker! Now, **that's** a bass!
PFFF!
Sadly out of your range!
Hmm...
Look. someone left their violin!
Dude! That's the o-r-i-gi-nal **McCartney** Beatles bass!
But surely you don't wanna get
Nooo!
Here, a **real** classic the Fender
Yeah... more like it!
not too common for you?

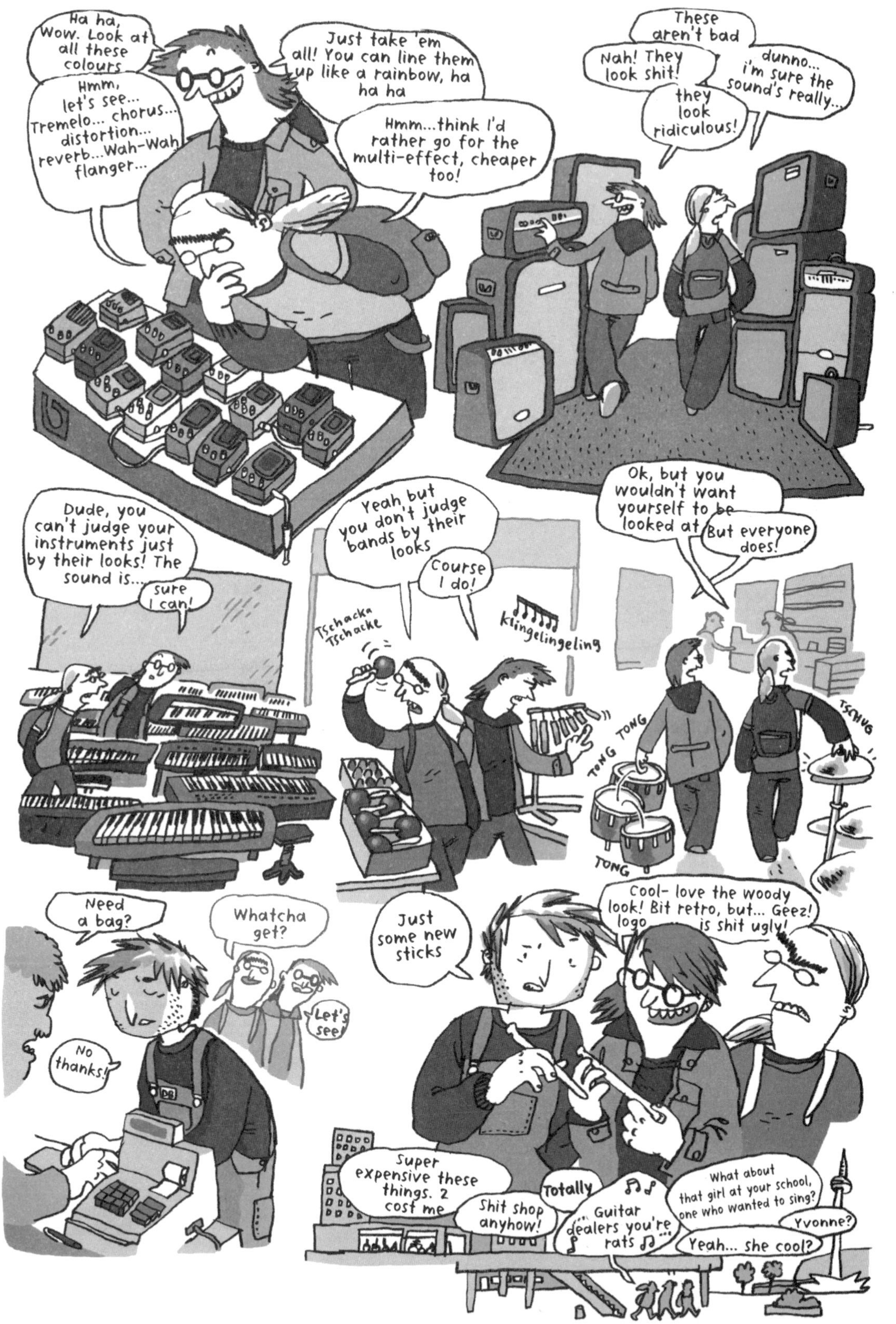
Ha ha, Wow. Look at all these colours
Hmm, let's see... Tremelo... chorus... distortion... reverb...Wah-Wah flanger...
Just take 'em all! You can line them up like a rainbow, ha ha ha
Hmm...think I'd rather go for the multi-effect, cheaper too!
These aren't bad
Nah! They look shit!
they look ridiculous!
dunno... i'm sure the sound's really...
Dude, you can't judge your instruments just by their looks! The sound is...
sure I can!
Yeah but you don't judge bands by their looks
Course I do!
Tschacka Tschacke
klingelingeling
Ok, but you wouldn't want yourself to be looked at
But everyone does!
TONG TONG
TONG
TSCHUG
Need a bag?
No thanks!
Whatcha get?
Let's see!
Just some new sticks
Cool- love the woody look! Bit retro, but... Geez! logo is shit ugly!
Super expensive these things. 2 cost me
Shit shop anyhow!
Totally
Guitar dealers you're rats
What about that girl at your school, one who wanted to sing?
Yvonne?
Yeah... she cool?

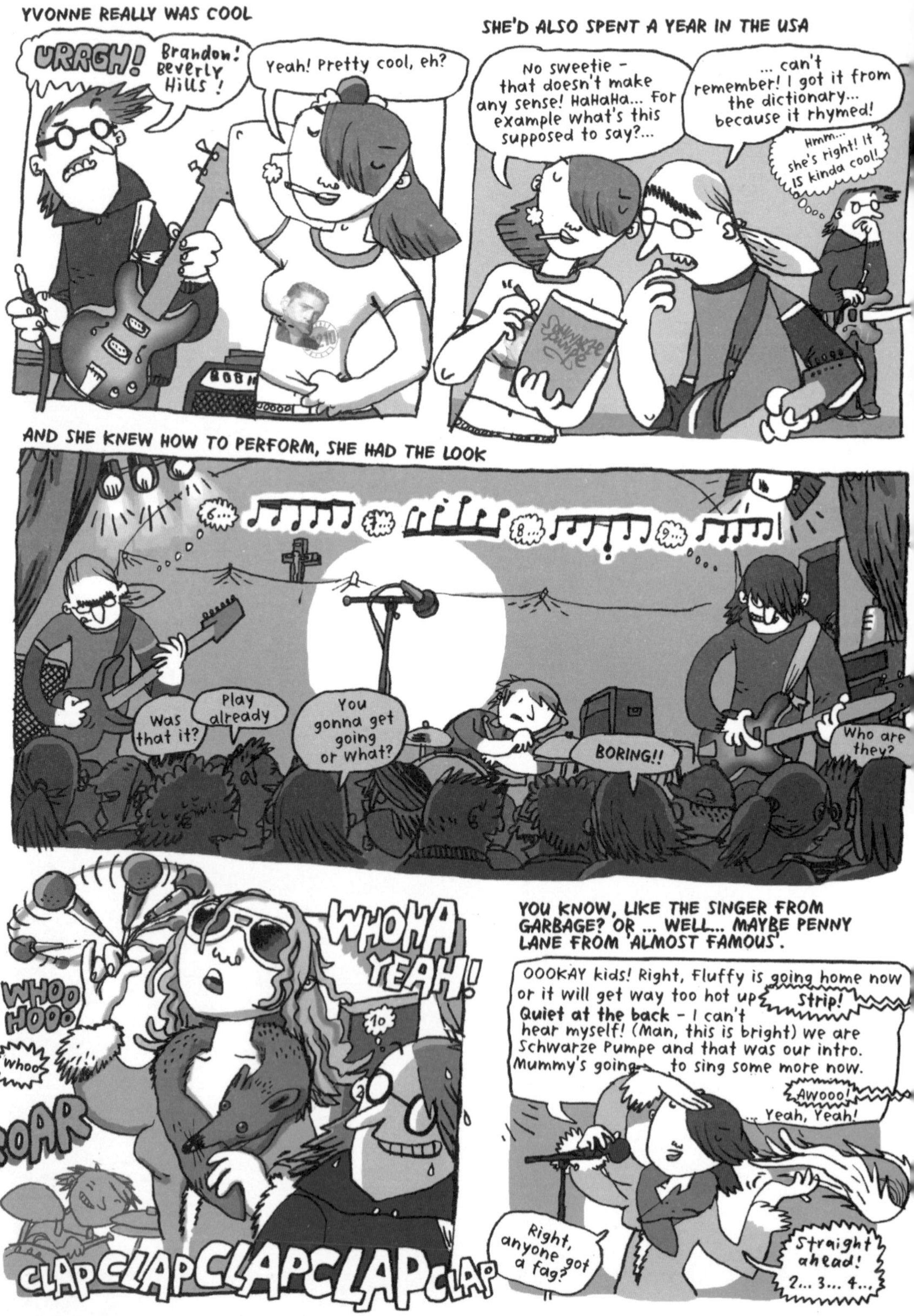

YVONNE REALLY WAS COOL
URRGH!
Brandon! Beverly Hills!
Yeah! Pretty cool, eh?
SHE'D ALSO SPENT A YEAR IN THE USA
No sweetie - that doesn't make any sense! HaHaHa... For example what's this supposed to say?...
... can't remember! I got it from the dictionary... because it rhymed!
Hmm... she's right! It IS kinda cool!
Schwarze Pumpe
AND SHE KNEW HOW TO PERFORM, SHE HAD THE LOOK
6...
7...
8...
9...
Was that it?
Play already
You gonna get going or what?
BORING!!
Who are they?
WHOHA YEAH!
10
WHOO HOOO
Whoo
ROAR
CLAP CLAP CLAP CLAP CLAP CLAP
YOU KNOW, LIKE THE SINGER FROM GARBAGE? OR ... WELL... MAYBE PENNY LANE FROM 'ALMOST FAMOUS'.
OOOKAY kids! Right, Fluffy is going home now or it will get way too hot up
Strip!
Quiet at the back - I can't hear myself! (Man, this is bright) we are Schwarze Pumpe and that was our intro. Mummy's going to sing some more now.
Awooo!
... Yeah, Yeah!
Right, anyone got a fag?
Straight ahead! 2... 3... 4...

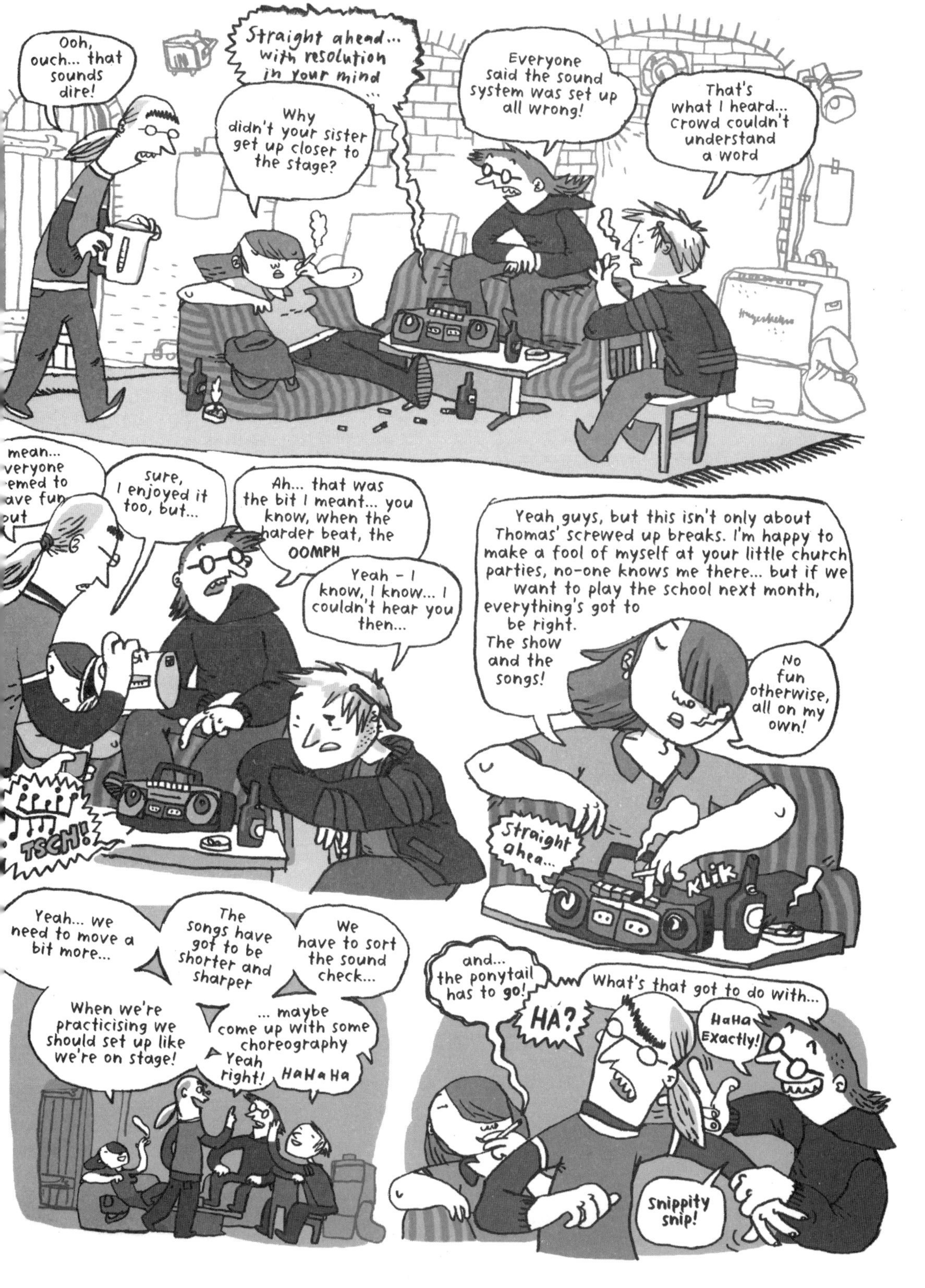
Ooh, ouch... that sounds dire!
Straight ahead... with resolution in your mind ...
Why didn't your sister get up closer to the stage?
Everyone said the sound system was set up all wrong!
That's what I heard... crowd couldn't understand a word
mean... veryone emed to ave fun out
sure, I enjoyed it too, but...
Ah... that was the bit I meant... you know, when the harder beat, the OOMPH
Yeah - I know, I know... I couldn't hear you then...
TSCH!
Yeah guys, but this isn't only about Thomas' screwed up breaks. I'm happy to make a fool of myself at your little church parties, no-one knows me there... but if we want to play the school next month, everything's got to be right. The show and the songs!
No fun otherwise, all on my own!
Straight ahea...
KLIK
Yeah... we need to move a bit more...
The songs have got to be shorter and sharper
We have to sort the sound check...
When we're practicising we should set up like we're on stage!
... maybe come up with some choreography
Yeah right!
HaHaHa
and... the ponytail has to go!
What's that got to do with...
HA?
HaHa Exactly!
Snippity snip!

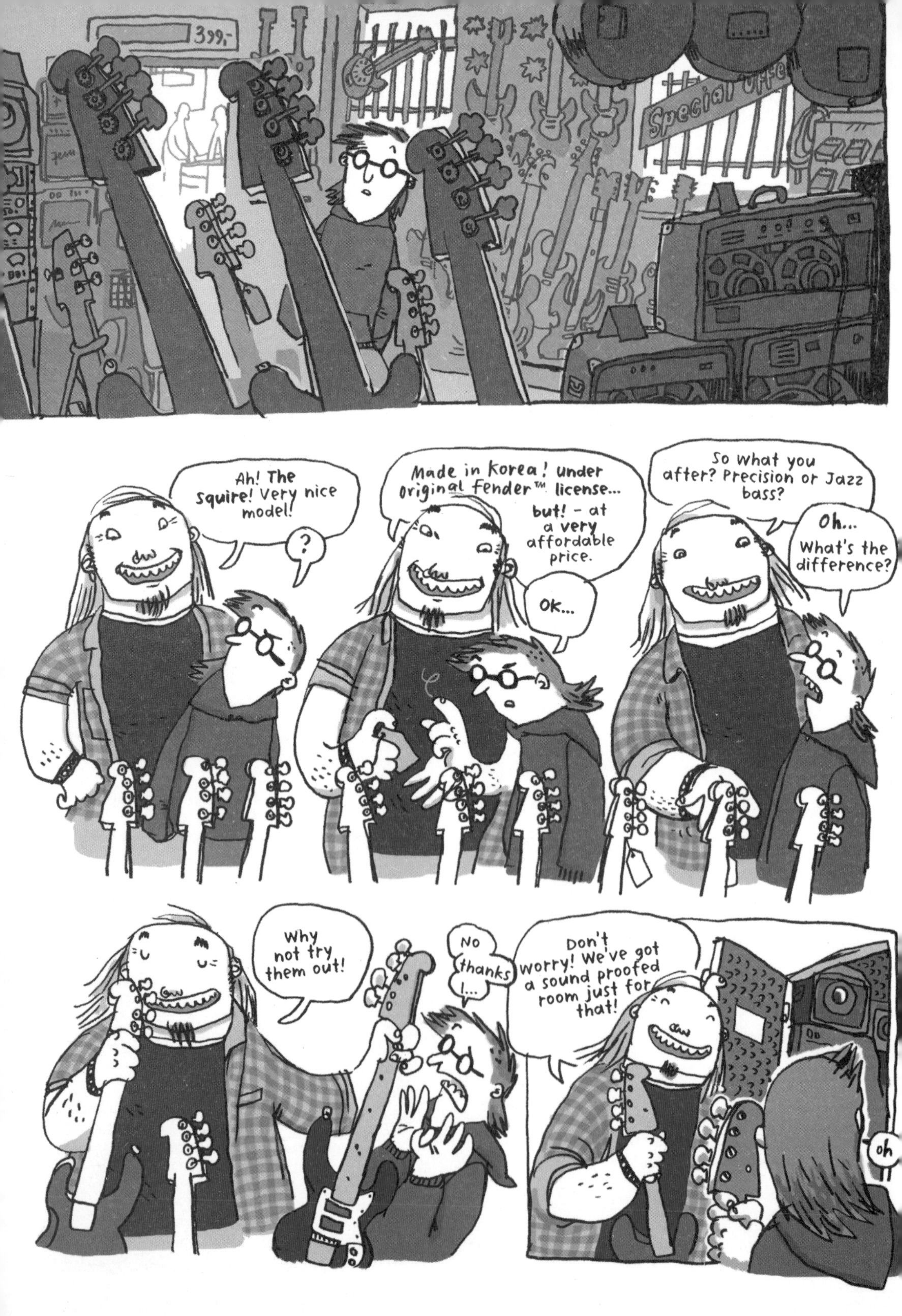
399,-
Special offer
Ah! The Squire! Very nice model!
?
Made in Korea! under original Fender™ license...
but! - at a very affordable price.
OK...
So what you after? Precision or Jazz bass?
Oh...
What's the difference?
Why not try them out!
No thanks I...
Don't worry! We've got a sound proofed room just for that!
oh

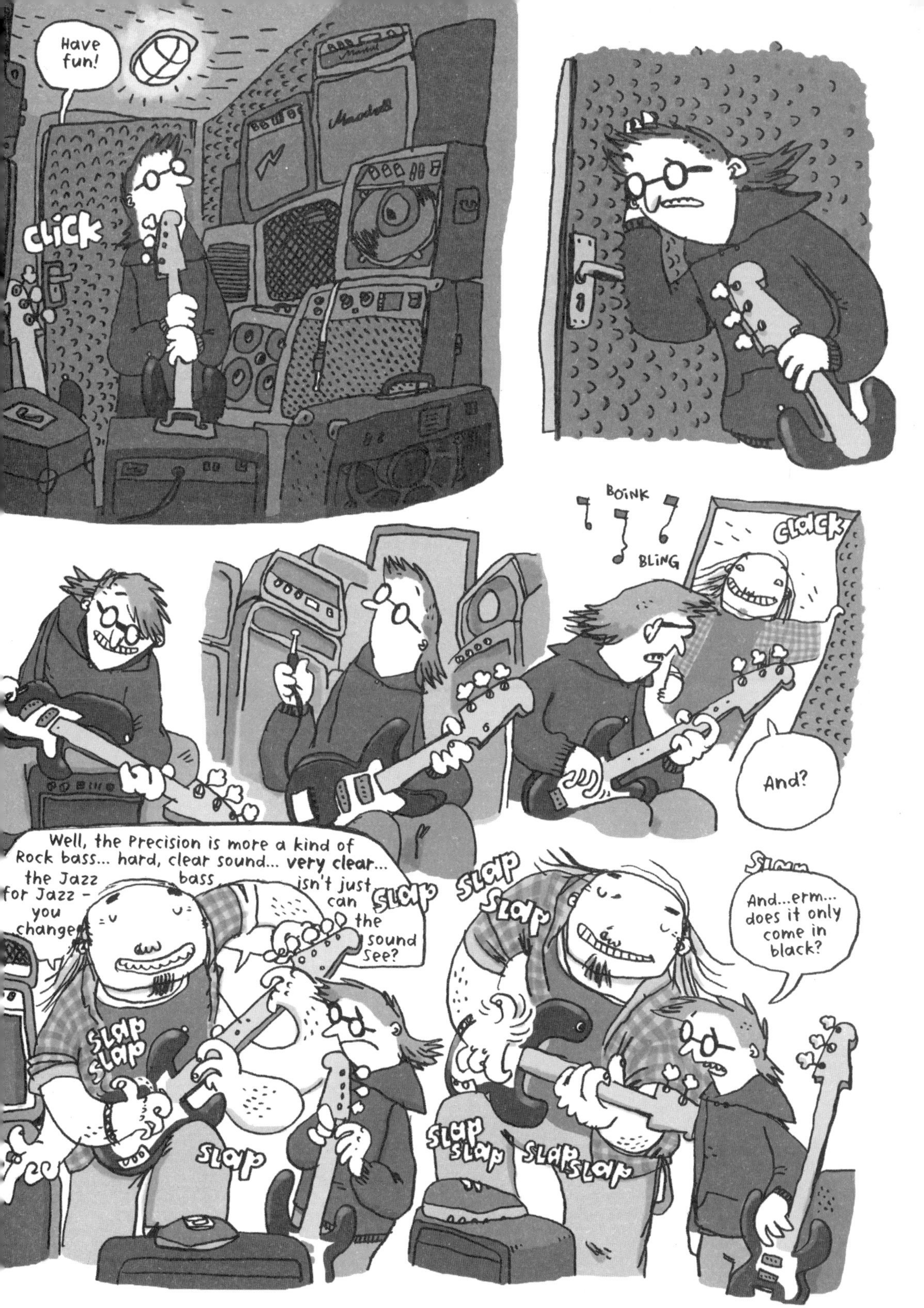

Have fun!
CLICK
BOINK
BLING
CLACK
And?
Well, the Precision is more a kind of Rock bass... hard, clear sound... very clear... the Jazz bass isn't just for Jazz - you can change the sound see?
SLAP
SLAP
SLAP
SLAP SLAP
SLAP
SLAP SLAP
SLAP SLAP
And...erm... does it only come in black?

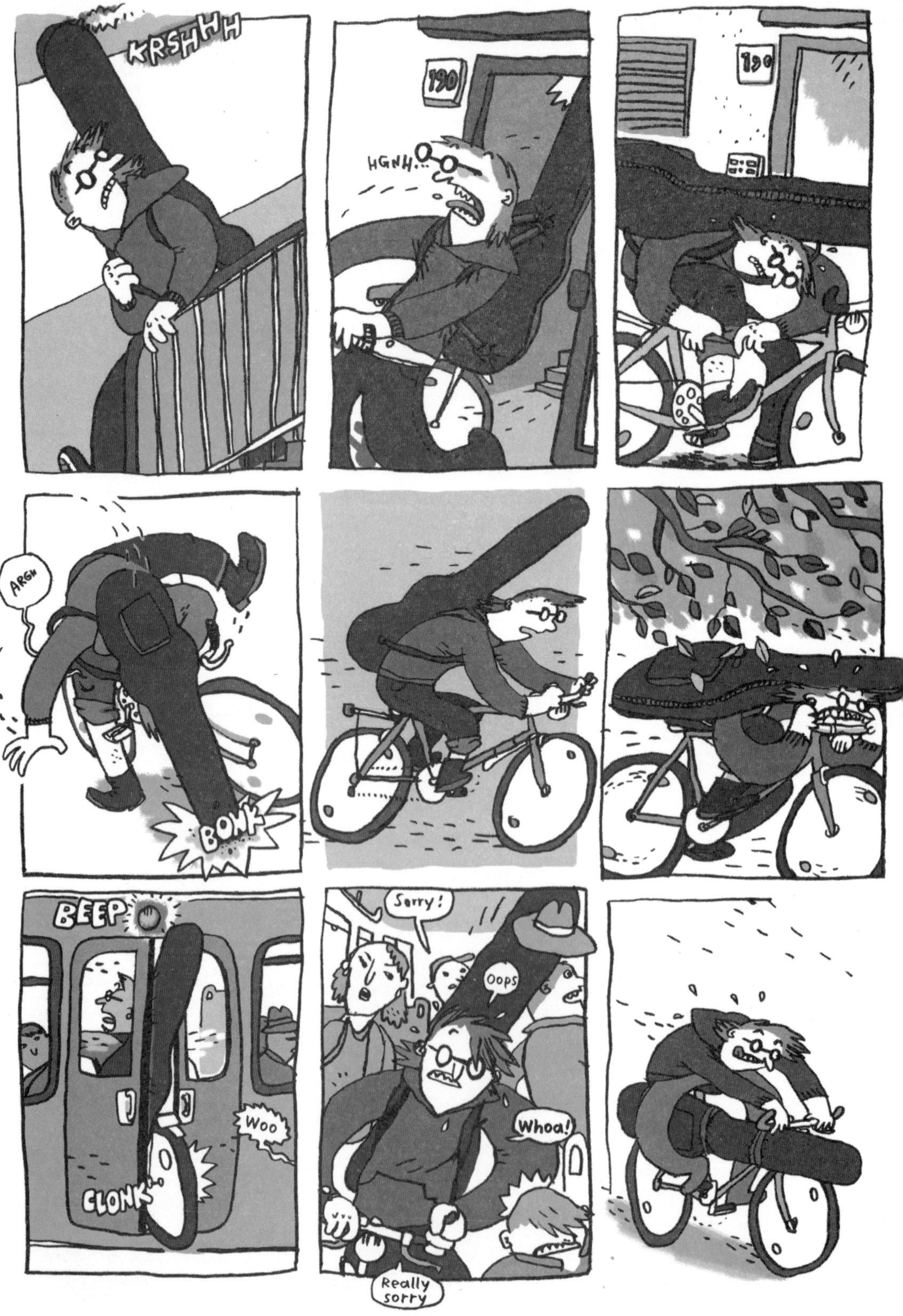
KRSHHH
HGNH...
ARGW
BONK
BEEP
Woo
CLONK
Sorry!
Oops
Whoa!
Really sorry

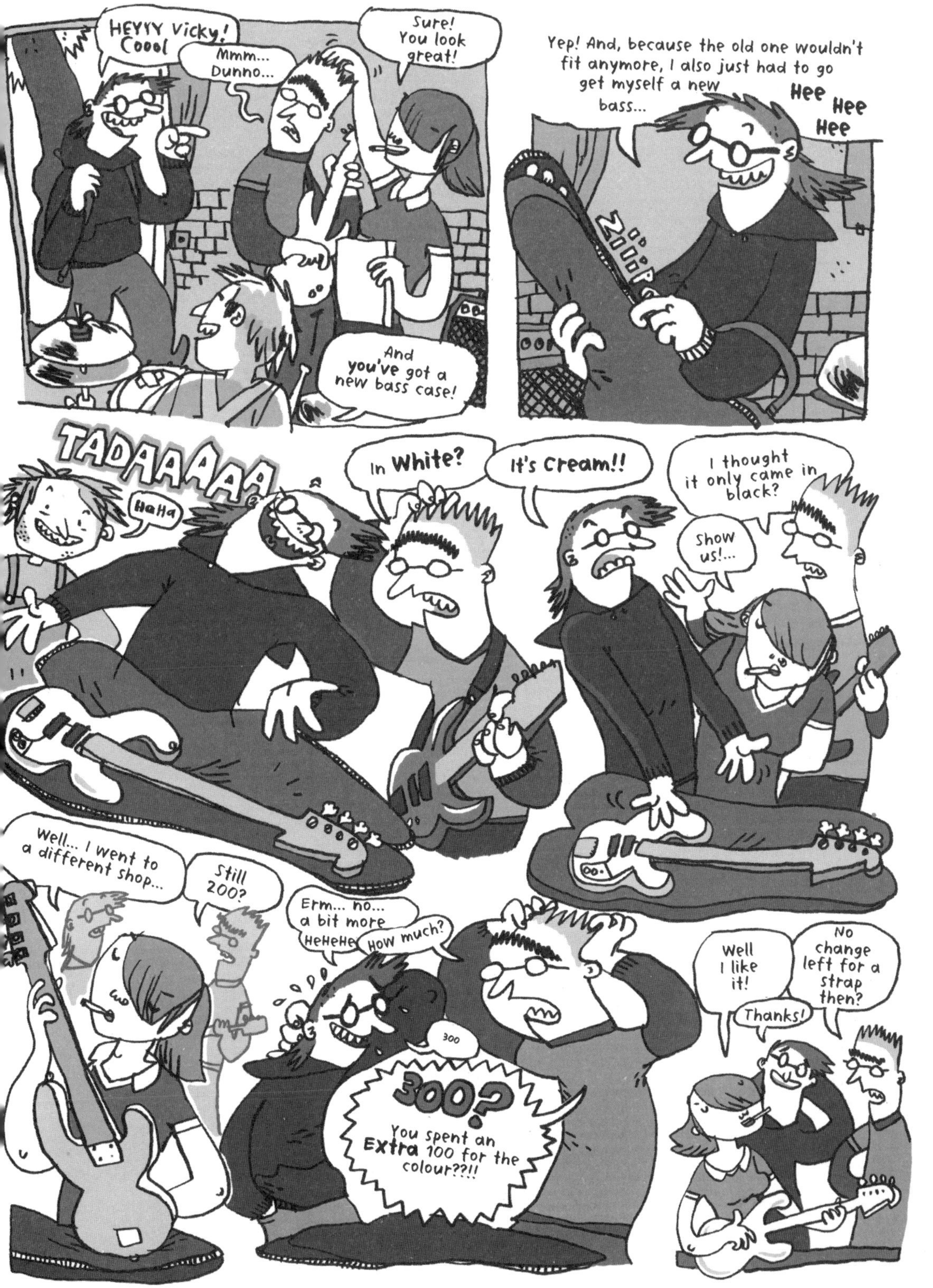

HEYYY Vicky! Coool
Mmm... Dunno...
Sure! You look great!
And you've got a new bass case!
Yep! And, because the old one wouldn't fit anymore, I also just had to go get myself a new bass...
Hee Hee Hee
ZOOOP
TADAAAAAA
HaHa
In White?
It's Cream!!
I thought it only came in black?
Show us!...
Well... I went to a different shop...
Still 200?
Erm... no... a bit more HeHeHe
How much?
300
300? You spent an Extra 100 for the colour??!!
Well I like it!
Thanks!
No change left for a strap then?

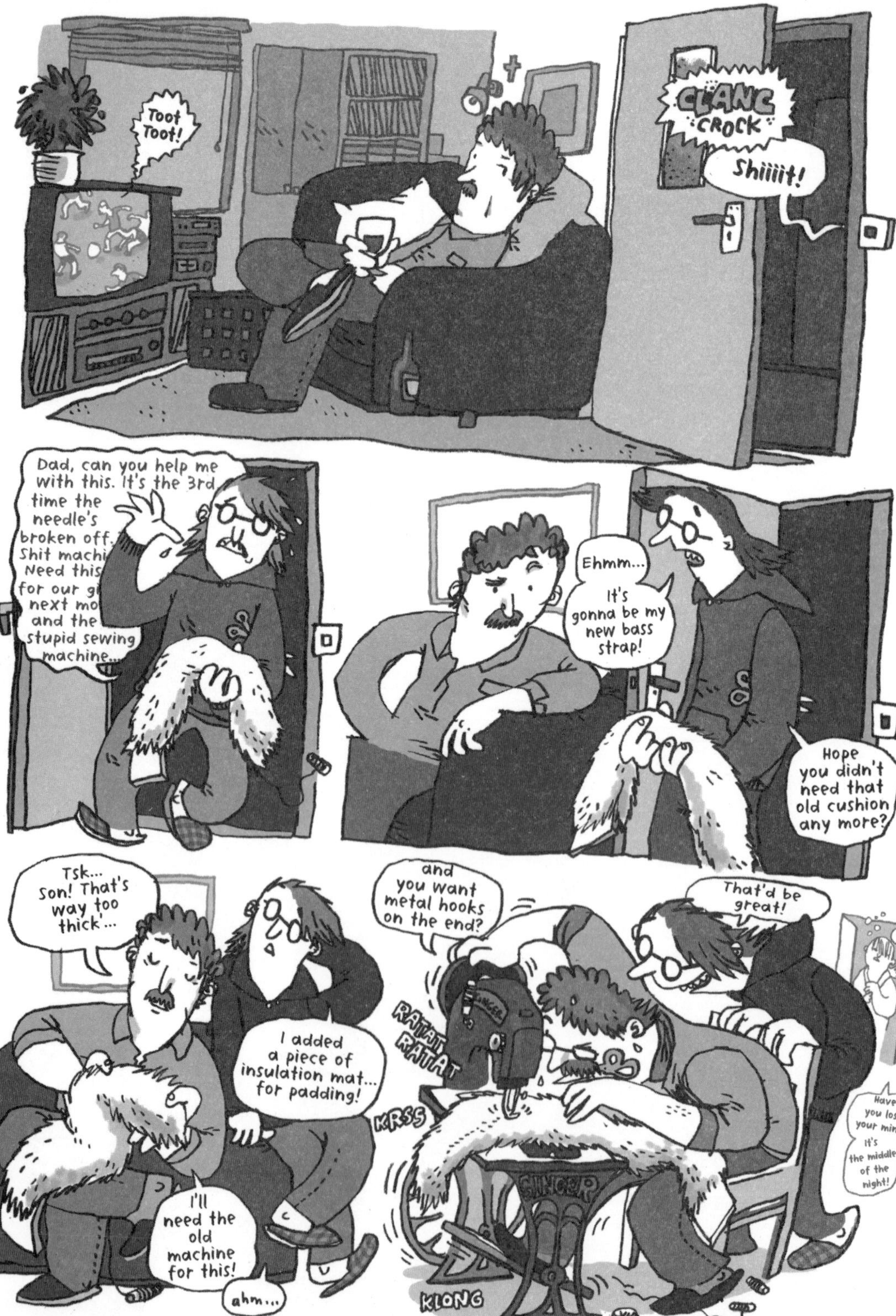

Toot Toot!
CLANG
CROCK
Shiiiit!
Dad, can you help me with this. It's the 3rd time the needle's broken off. Shit machi Need this for our gi next mo and the stupid sewing machine...
Ehmm...
It's gonna be my new bass strap!
Hope you didn't need that old cushion any more?
Tsk... Son! That's way too thick'...
I added a piece of insulation mat... for padding!
I'll need the old machine for this!
ahm...
and you want metal hooks on the end?
That'd be great!
RATATAT
RATATAT
KRSS
SINGER
KLONG
Have you lost your minds It's the middle of the night!

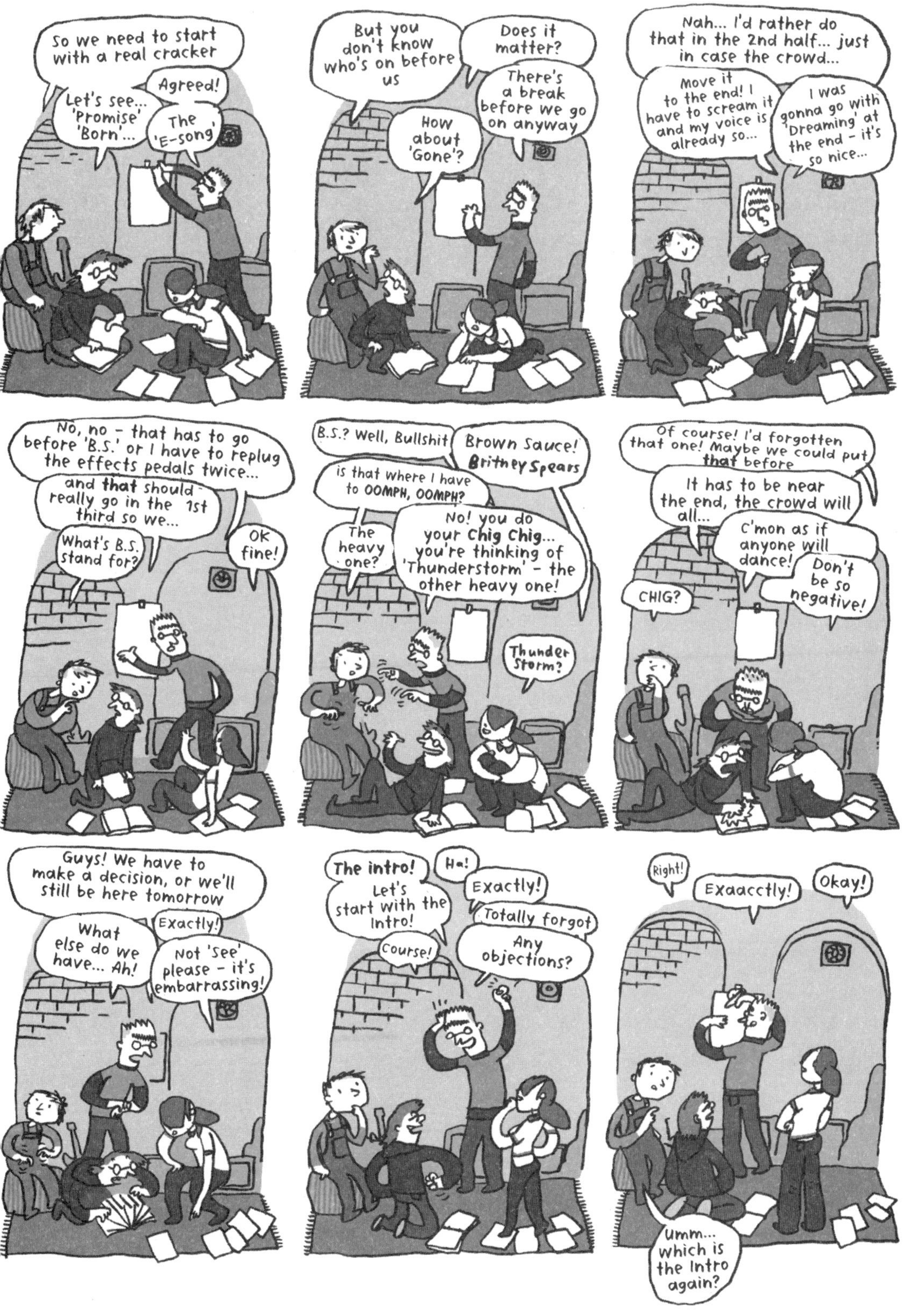
So we need to start with a real cracker
Agreed!
Let's see... 'Promise' 'Born'...
The 'E-song'
But you don't know who's on before us
Does it matter?
There's a break before we go on anyway
How about 'Gone'?
Nah... I'd rather do that in the 2nd half... just in case the crowd...
Move it to the end! I have to scream it and my voice is already so...
I was gonna go with 'Dreaming' at the end - it's so nice...
No, no - that has to go before 'B.S.' or I have to replug the effects pedals twice...
and **that** should really go in the 1st third so we...
What's B.S. stand for?
OK fine!
B.S.? Well, Bullshit
Brown Sauce! **Britney Spears**
is that where I have to OOMPH, OOMPH?
The heavy one?
No! you do your **Chig Chig**... you're thinking of 'Thunderstorm' - the other heavy one!
Thunder Storm?
Of course! I'd forgotten that one! Maybe we could put **that** before
It has to be near the end, the crowd will all...
C'mon as if anyone will dance!
Don't be so negative!
CHIG?
Guys! We have to make a decision, or we'll still be here tomorrow
What else do we have... Ah!
Exactly!
Not 'See' please - it's embarrassing!
The intro!
Ha!
Let's start with the Intro!
Exactly!
Totally forgot
Course!
Any objections?
Right!
Exaacctly!
Okay!
Umm... which is the Intro again?

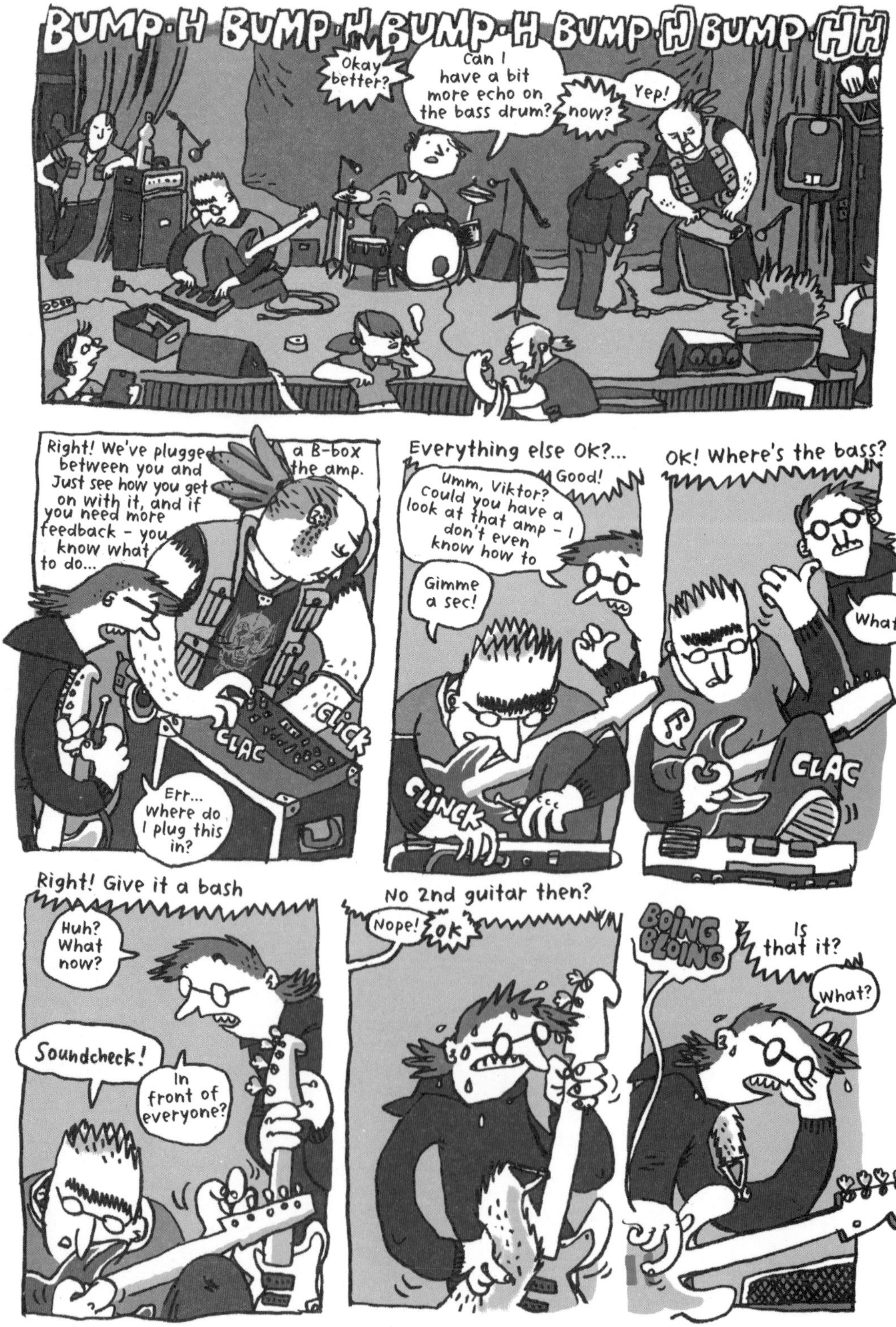
BUMP·H BUMP·H BUMP·H BUMP·(H) BUMP·(HH)
Okay better?
Can I have a bit more echo on the bass drum?
now?
Yep!
Right! We've plugged a B-box between you and the amp. Just see how you get on with it, and if you need more feedback - you know what to do...
CLAC
CLICK
Err... where do I plug this in?
Everything else OK?...
Good!
Umm, Viktor? Could you have a look at that amp - I don't even know how to
Gimme a sec!
CLINCK
OK! Where's the bass?
What?
CLAC
Right! Give it a bash
Huh? What now?
Soundcheck!
In front of everyone?
No 2nd guitar then?
Nope!
OK
BOING BLOING
Is that it?
What?

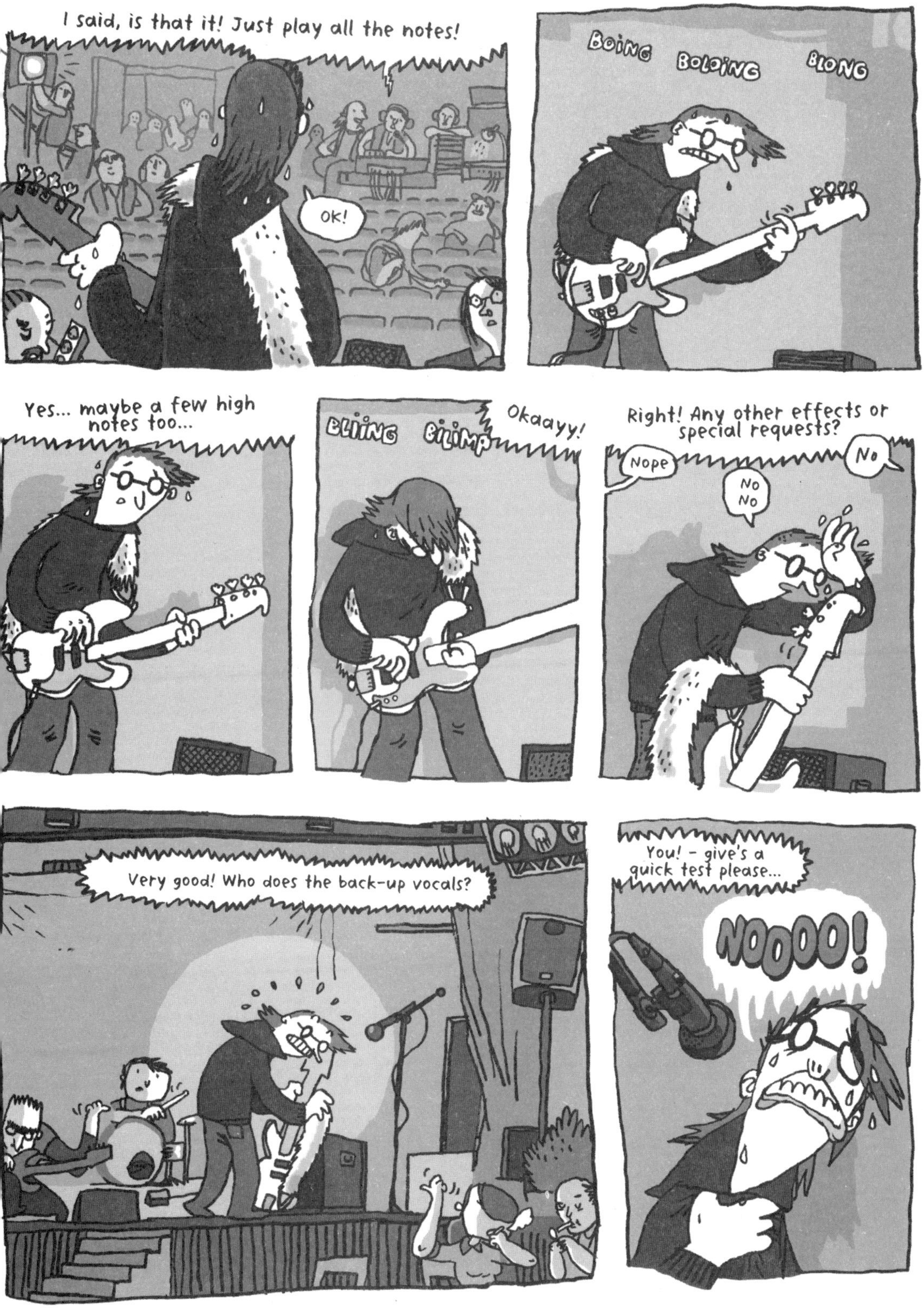
I said, is that it! Just play all the notes!
OK!
BOING BOLOING BLONG
Yes... maybe a few high notes too...
BLIING BILIMP
Okaayy!
Right! Any other effects or special requests?
Nope
No No
No
Very good! Who does the back-up vocals?
You! - give's a quick test please...
NOOOO!

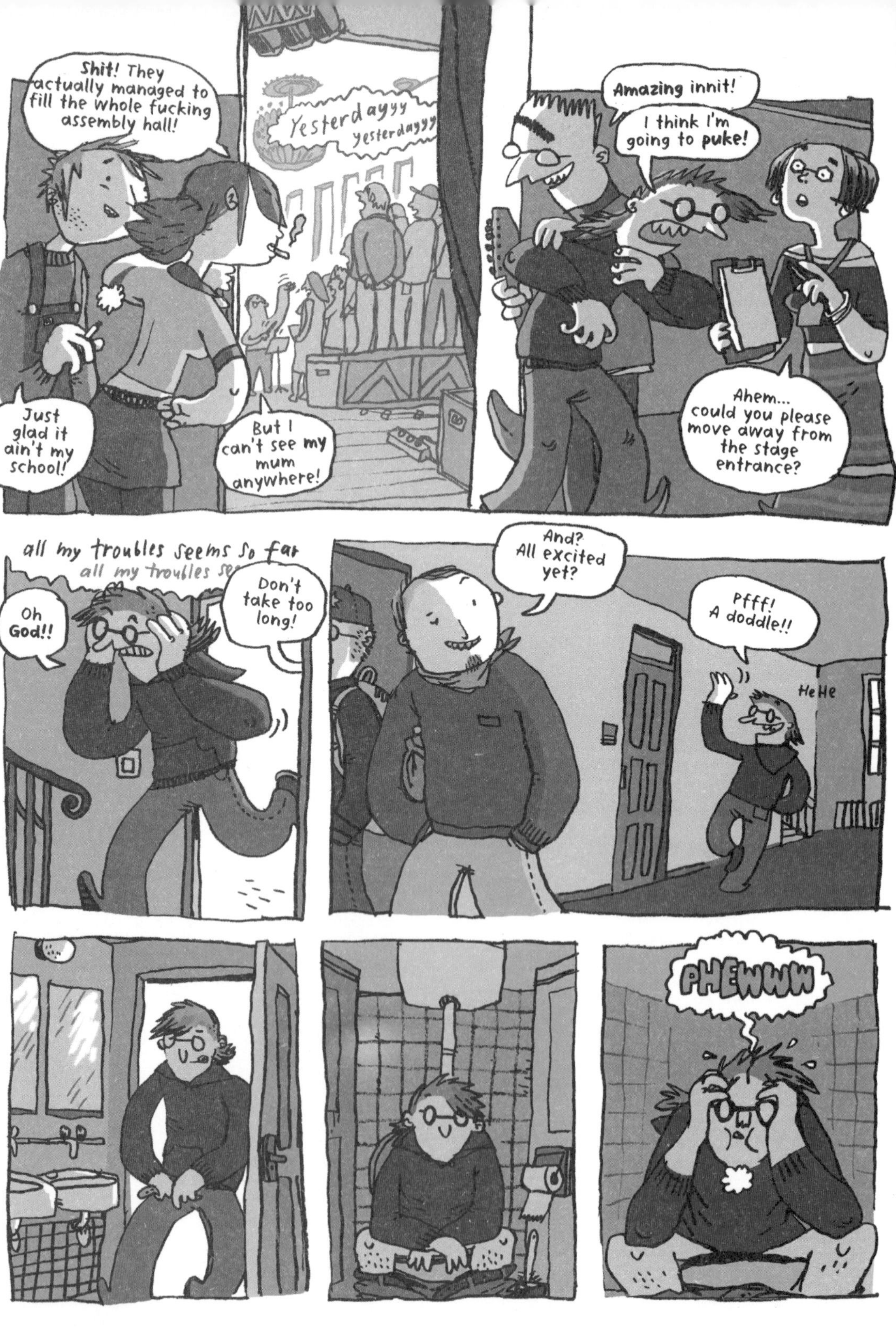
Shit! They actually managed to fill the whole fucking assembly hall!
Yesterdayyy yesterdayyy
Just glad it ain't my school!
But I can't see my mum anywhere!
Amazing innit!
I think I'm going to puke!
Ahem... could you please move away from the stage entrance?
all my troubles seems so far
all my troubles se
Oh God!!
Don't take too long!
And? All excited yet?
Pfff! A doddle!!
HeHe
PHEWWW

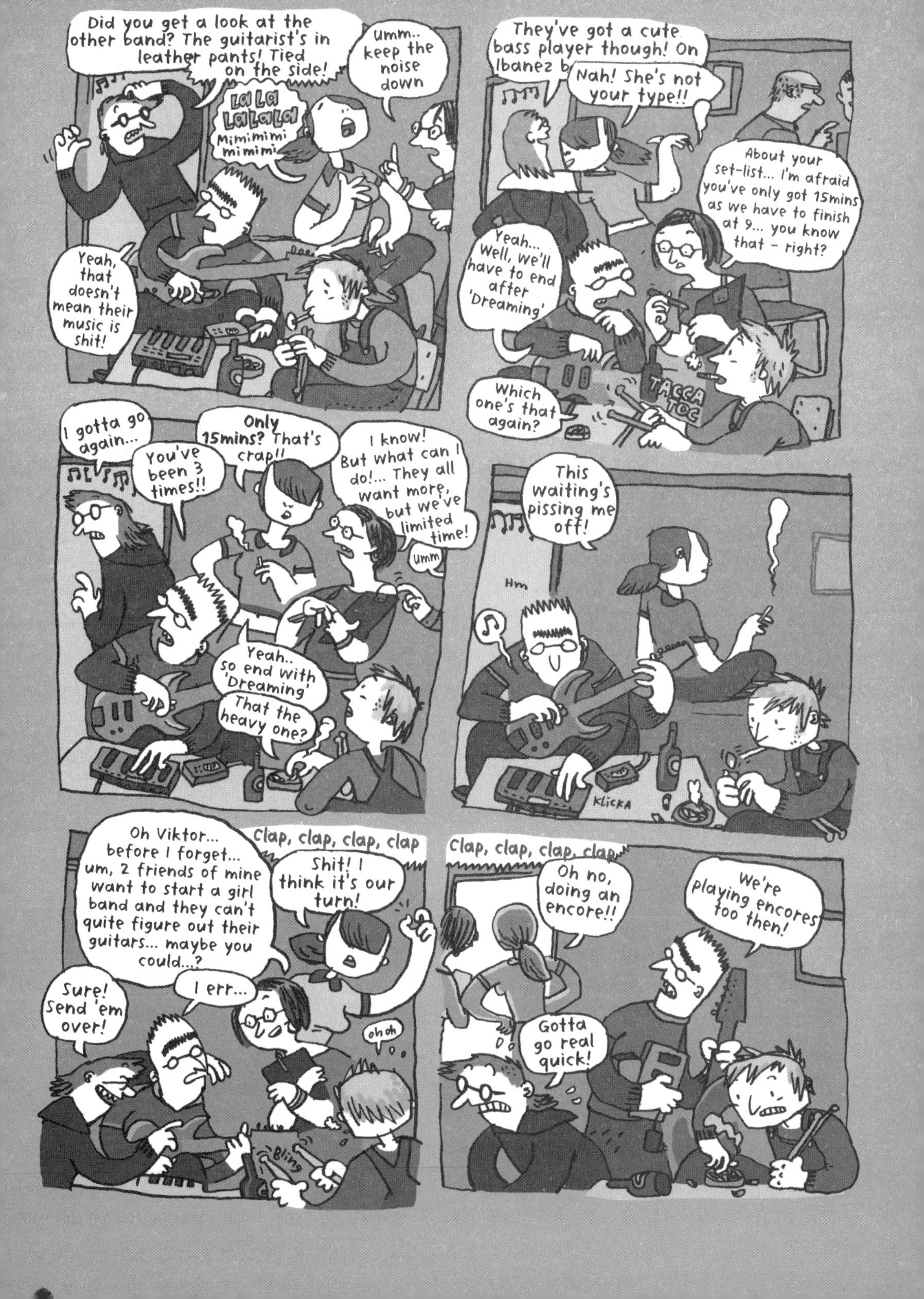

Did you get a look at the other band? The guitarist's in leather pants! Tied on the side!
umm.. keep the noise down
La La LaLaLa
Mimimimi mimimi
Yeah, that doesn't mean their music is shit!
They've got a cute bass player though! On Ibanez b
Nah! She's not your type!!
About your set-list... I'm afraid you've only got 15mins as we have to finish at 9... you know that - right?
Yeah... Well, we'll have to end after 'Dreaming'
Which one's that again?
TACCA TOC
I gotta go again...
You've been 3 times!!
Only 15mins? That's crap!!
I know! But what can I do!... They all want more, but we've limited time!
umm
Yeah.. so end with 'Dreaming'
That the heavy one?
This waiting's pissing me off!
Hm
KLICKA
Oh Viktor... before I forget... um, 2 friends of mine want to start a girl band and they can't quite figure out their guitars... maybe you could...?
Clap, clap, clap, clap
Shit! I think it's our turn!
Sure! Send 'em over!
I err...
oh oh
Bling
Clap, clap, clap, clap
Oh no, doing an encore!!
We're playing encores too then!
Gotta go real quick!

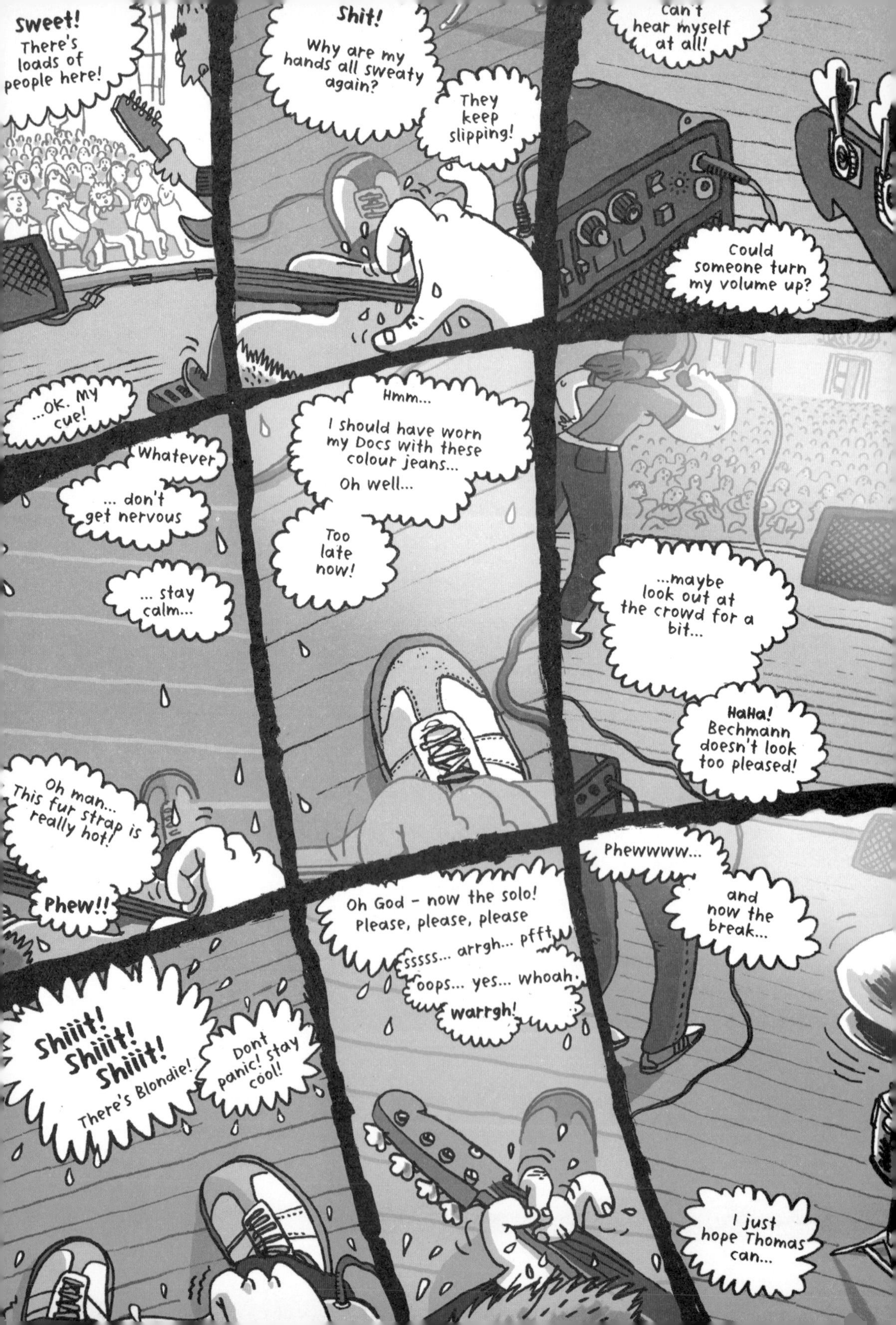

Sweet! There's loads of people here!
Shit! Why are my hands all sweaty again?
They keep slipping!
can't hear myself at all!
Could someone turn my volume up?
...OK. My cue!
Whatever
... don't get nervous
... stay calm...
Hmm... I should have worn my Docs with these colour jeans... Oh well...
Too late now!
...maybe look out at the crowd for a bit...
HaHa! Bechmann doesn't look too pleased!
Oh man... This fur strap is really hot!
Phew!!
Oh God - now the solo! Please, please, please
sssss... arrgh... pfft
oops... yes... whoah.
warrgh!
Phewwww...
and now the break...
Shiiit! Shiiit! Shiiit! There's Blondie!
Dont panic! stay cool!
I just hope Thomas can...

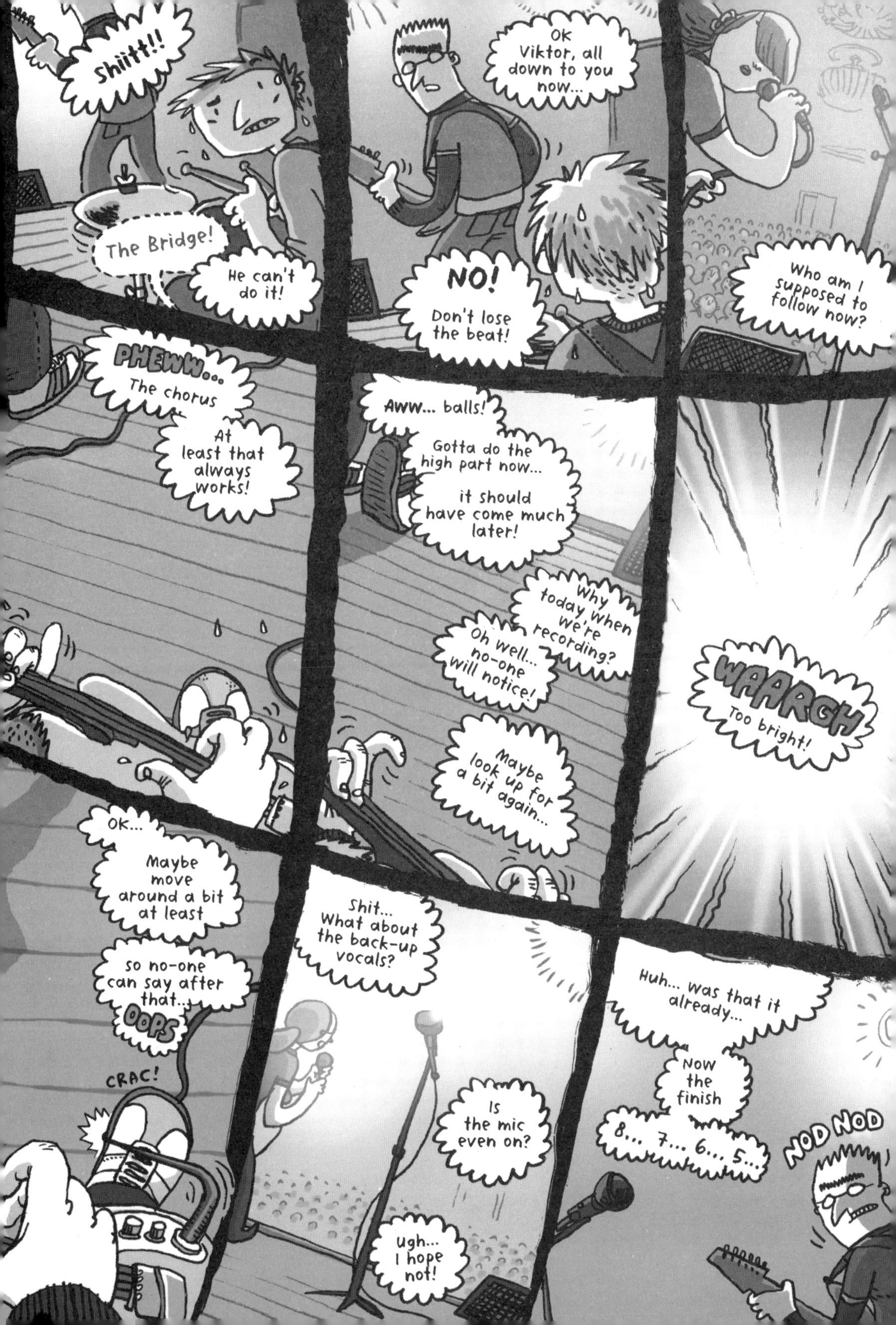

Shiitt!!
The Bridge!
He can't do it!
OK Viktor, all down to you now...
NO! Don't lose the beat!
Who am I supposed to follow now?
PHEWW... The chorus
At least that always works!
AWW... balls!
Gotta do the high part now...
it should have come much later!
Why today, when we're recording?
Oh well... no-one will notice!
Maybe look up for a bit again...
WAARGH Too bright!
OK...
Maybe move around a bit at least
so no-one can say after that...
OOPS
CRAC!
Shit... What about the back-up vocals?
Is the mic even on?
Ugh... I hope not!
Huh... was that it already...
Now the finish
8... 7... 6... 5...
NOD NOD

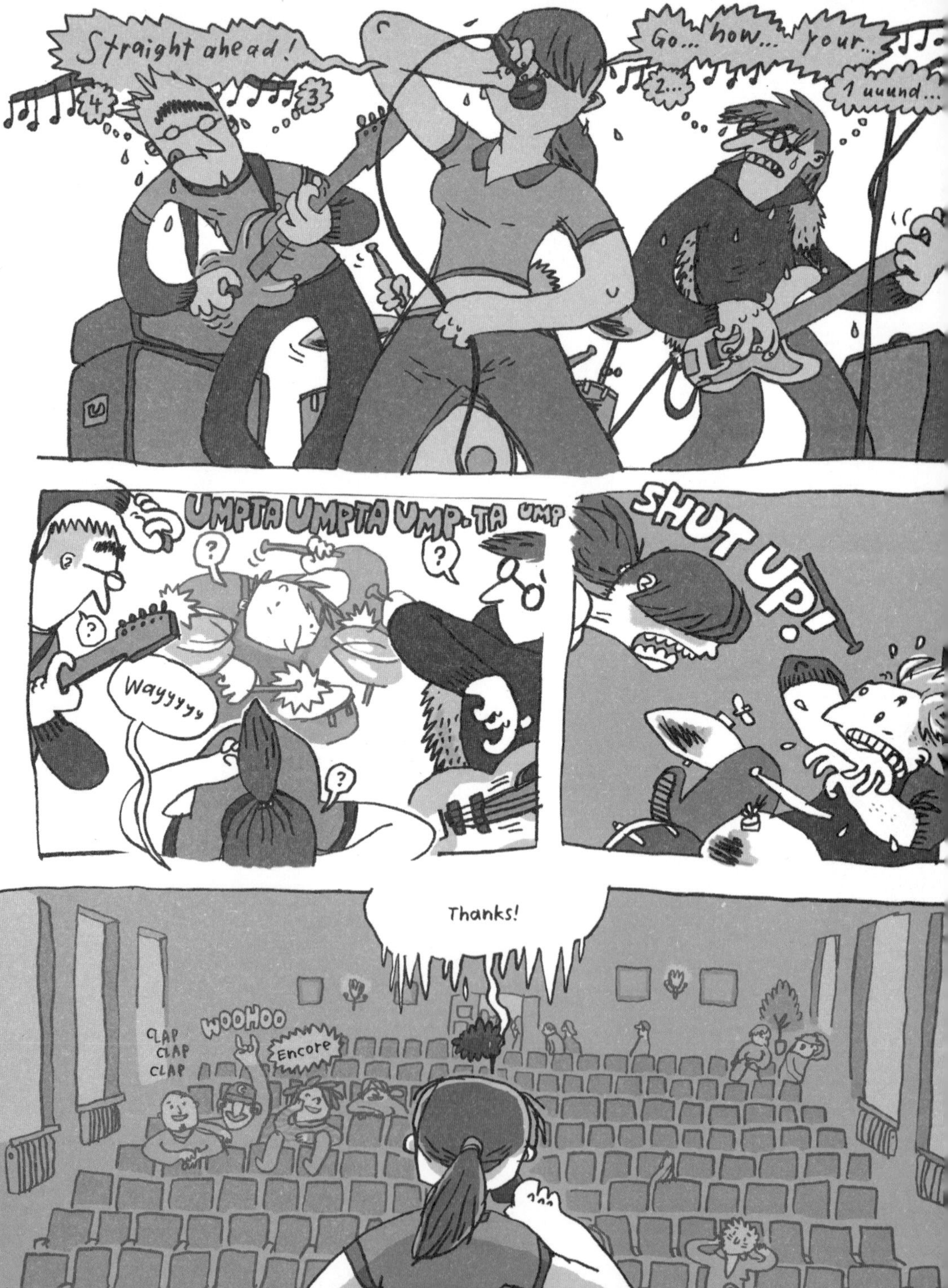
Straight ahead!
4
3
Go... how... your...
2...
1 uuund...
UMPTA UMPTA UMP-TA UMP
?
?
?
?
Wayyyyy
SHUT UP!
Thanks!
CLAP
CLAP
CLAP
WOOHOO
Encore

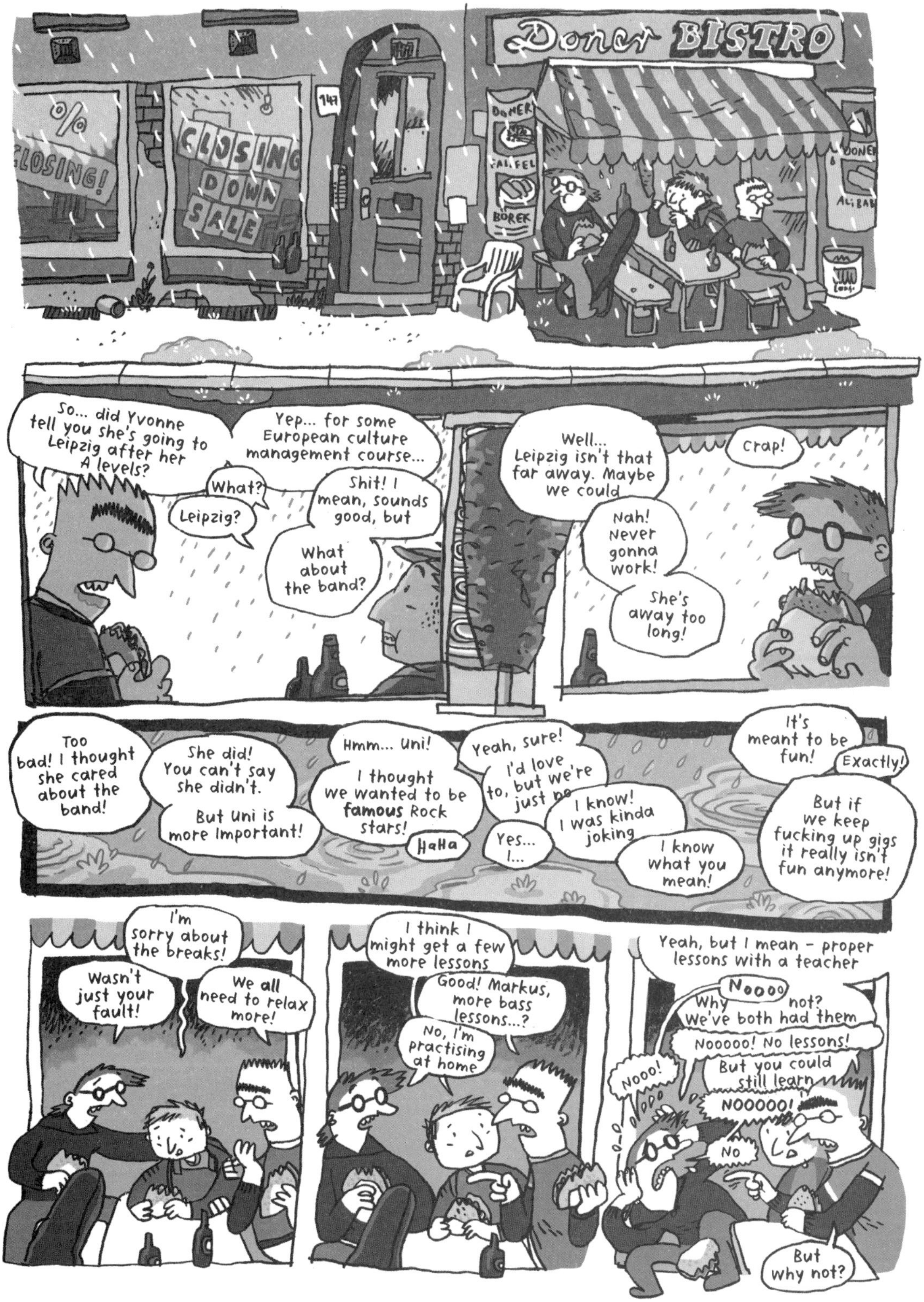
Doner BISTRO
CLOSING!
CLOSING DOWN SALE
DONER
FALAFEL
BÖREK
So... did Yvonne tell you she's going to Leipzig after her A levels?
Yep... for some European culture management course...
What?
Leipzig?
Shit! I mean, sounds good, but
What about the band?
Well... Leipzig isn't that far away. Maybe we could
Crap!
Nah! Never gonna work!
She's away too long!
Too bad! I thought she cared about the band!
She did! You can't say she didn't.
But Uni is more important!
Hmm... Uni!
I thought we wanted to be famous Rock stars!
HaHa
Yeah, sure!
I'd love to, but we're just
Yes... I...
I know! I was kinda joking
I know what you mean!
It's meant to be fun!
Exactly!
But if we keep fucking up gigs it really isn't fun anymore!
I'm sorry about the breaks!
Wasn't just your fault!
We all need to relax more!
I think I might get a few more lessons
Good! Markus, more bass lessons...?
No, I'm practising at home
Yeah, but I mean - proper lessons with a teacher
Noooo
Why not? We've both had them
Nooooo! No lessons!
Nooo!
But you could still learn
NOOOOO!
NO
But why not?

MY PARENTS SENT ME TO PIANO LESSONS FOR THREE YEARS

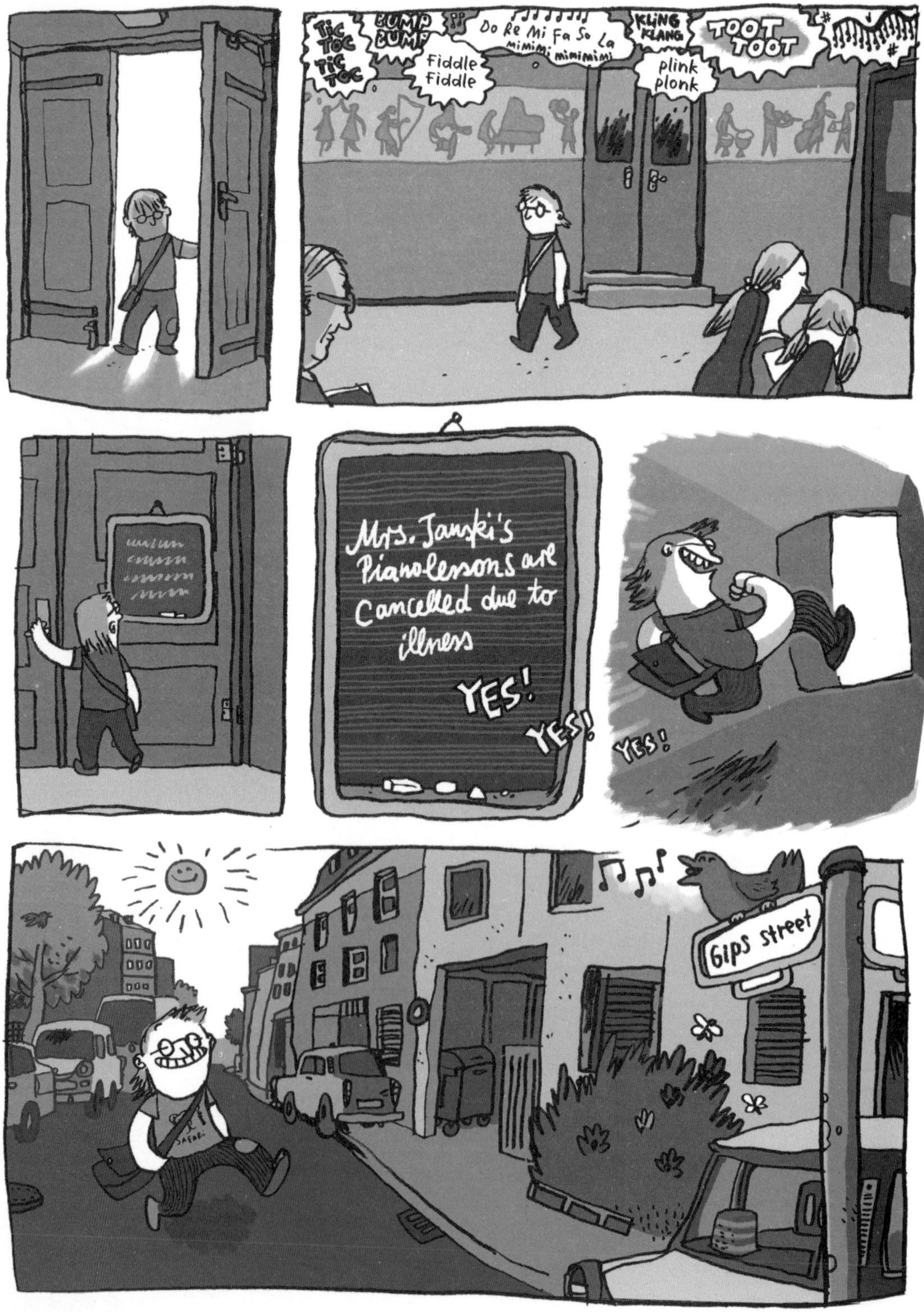

TIC TOC TIC TOC
BUMP BUMP
Do Re Mi Fa So La mimimi mimimimi
Fiddle Fiddle
KLING KLANG
plink plonk
TOOT TOOT
Mrs. Janski's Pianolessons are Cancelled due to illness
YES!
YES!
YES!
Gips street

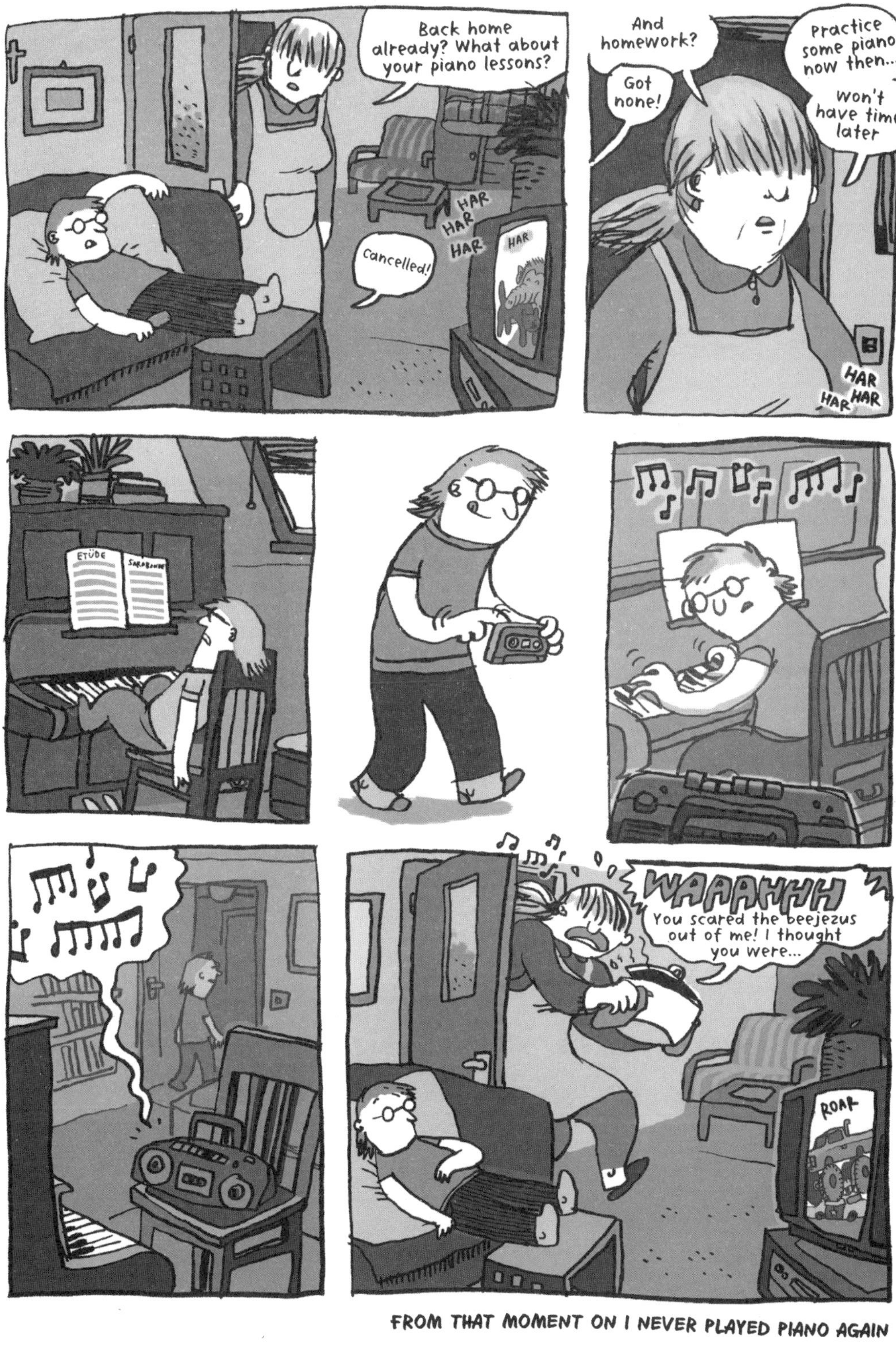
Back home already? What about your piano lessons?
HAR HAR HAR
HAR
Cancelled!
And homework?
Got none!
Practice some piano now then...
Won't have time later
HAR HAR HAR
ETÜDE
WAAAHHH
You scared the beejezus out of me! I thought you were...
ROAR

FROM THAT MOMENT ON I NEVER PLAYED PIANO AGAIN

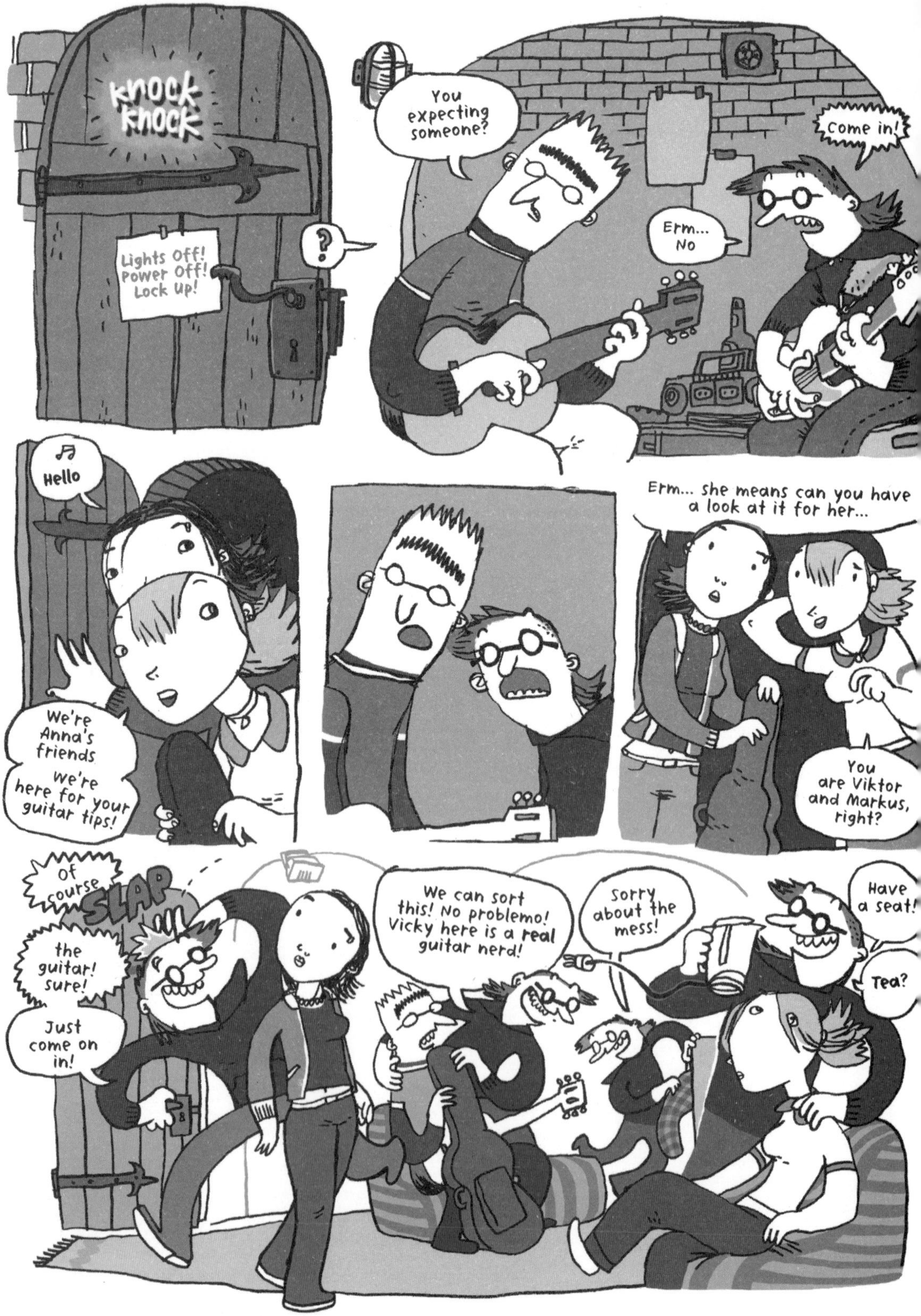
knock knock
Lights Off! Power Off! Lock Up!
?
You expecting someone?
Come in!
Erm... No
♫ Hello
We're Anna's friends
We're here for your guitar tips!
Erm... she means can you have a look at it for her...
You are Viktor and Markus, right?
Of course
SLAP
the guitar! sure!
Just come on in!
We can sort this! No problemo! Vicky here is a real guitar nerd!
Sorry about the mess!
Have a seat!
Tea?

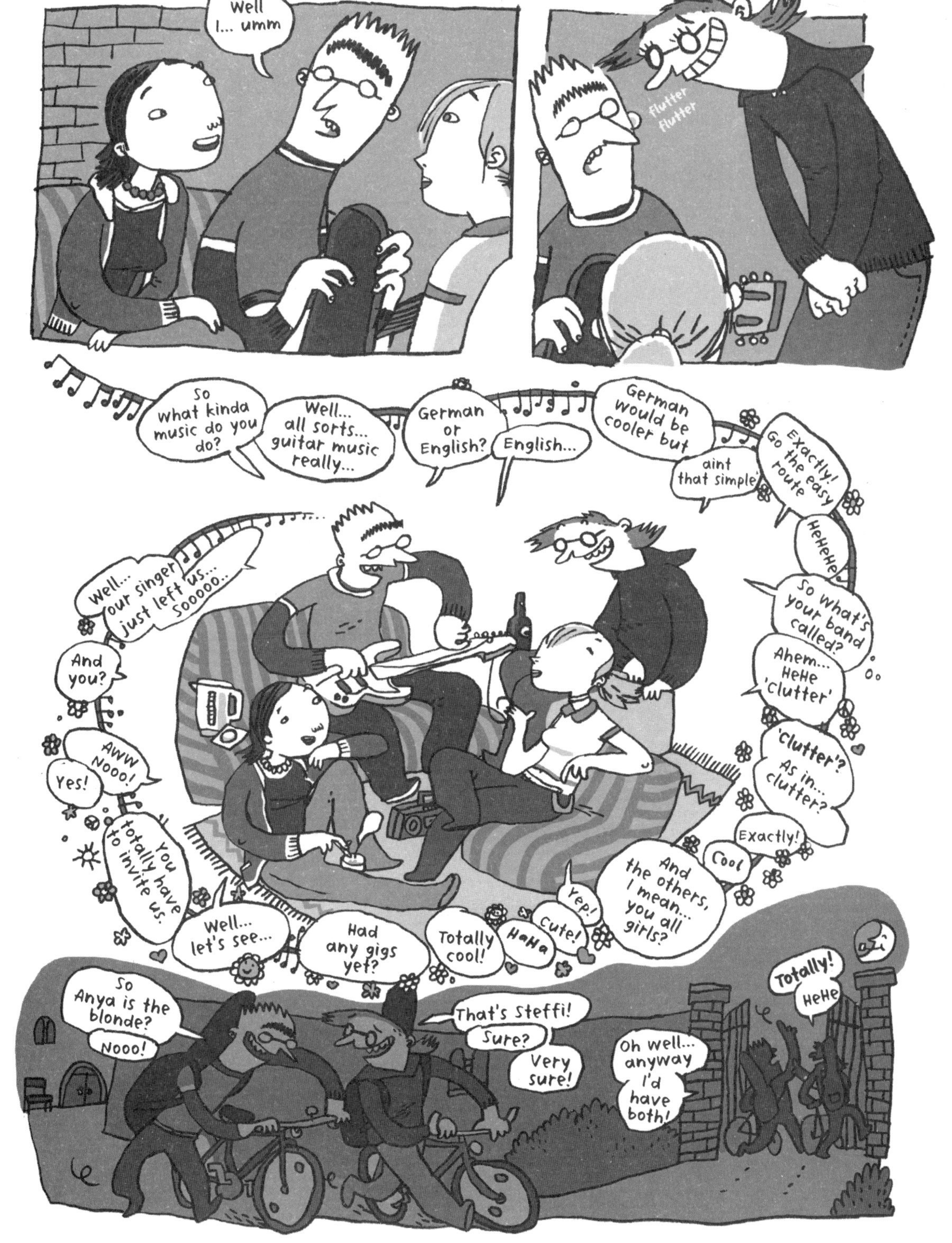

Well I... umm
Flutter Flutter
So what kinda music do you do?
Well... all sorts... guitar music really...
German or English?
English...
German would be cooler but
aint that simple
Exactly! Go the easy route
HeHeHe
Well... our singer just left us... Sooooo...
And you?
Aww Nooo!
Yes!
You totally have to invite us.
Well... let's see...
Had any gigs yet?
Totally cool!
HaHa
Cute!
Yep!
And the others, I mean... you all girls?
Cool
Exactly!
'Clutter'? As in... clutter?
Ahem... HeHe 'Clutter'
So what's your band called?
So Anya is the blonde?
Nooo!
That's Steffi!
Sure?
Very sure!
Oh well... anyway I'd have both!
Totally!
HeHe

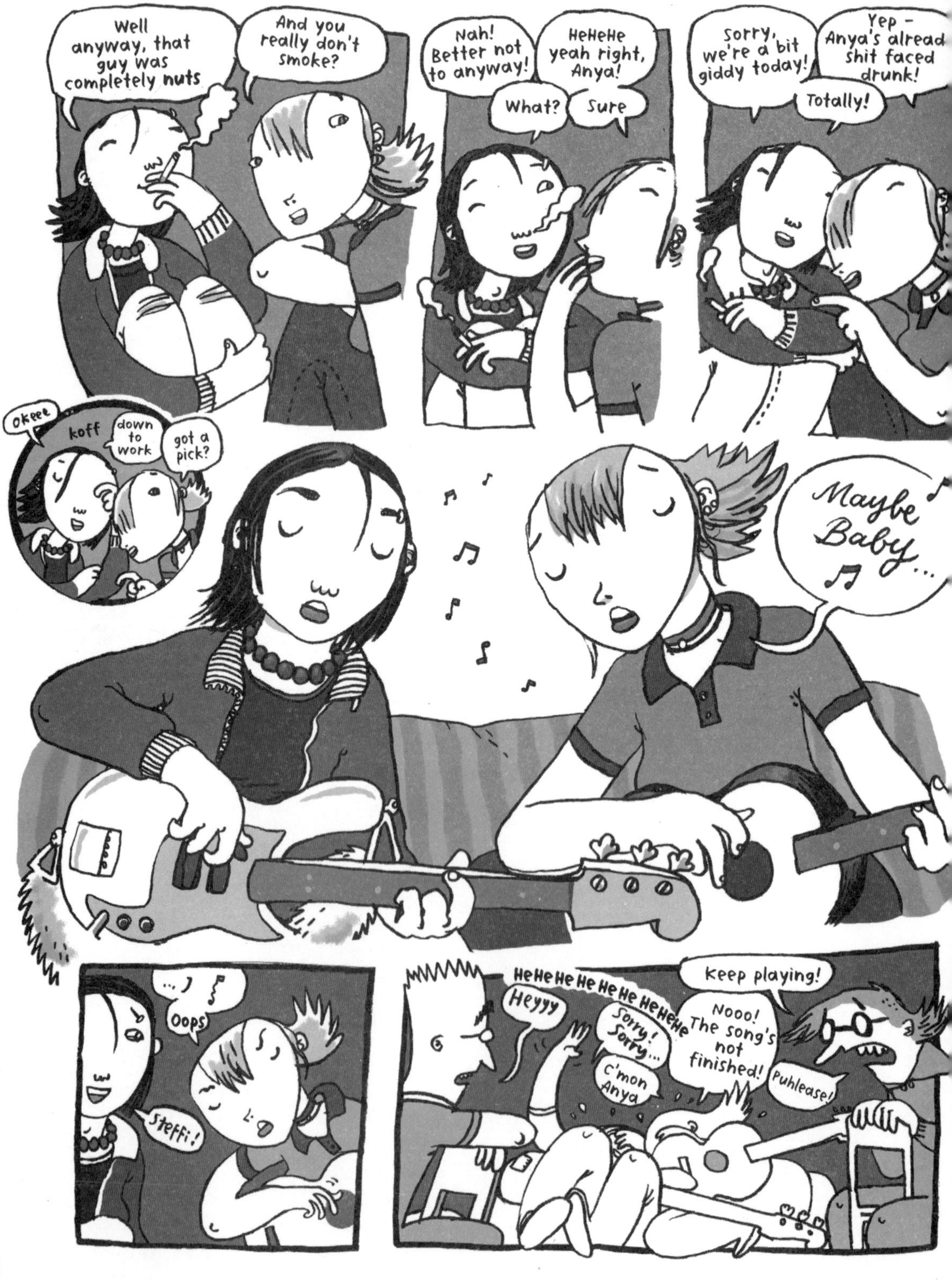

Well anyway, that guy was completely nuts
And you really don't smoke?
Nah! Better not to anyway!
HeHeHe yeah right, Anya!
What?
Sure
Sorry, we're a bit giddy today!
Yep - Anya's alread shit faced drunk!
Totally!
Okeee
koff
down to work
got a pick?
Maybe Baby...
...
Oops
Steffi!
HeHeHeHeHeHeHeHeHeHe
Heyyy
Sorry! Sorry...
C'mon Anya
Keep playing!
Nooo! The song's not finished!
Puhlease!

Can you teach me some bass?
Me?
But I'm... I'm not really very...
Go for it!
You're a lot more experienced at this ...
You think?
Why don't you show me some tricks
Tricks?
You know, fancy bass stuff
OKAY, well, for example... this tone here, erm... 2nd string here
A?
... err yeah A err... then
... then you can pull it like so to these 2 dots here...
An octave?
Erm... octave... exactly... could be... yeah...
or also... when you pull this string down and then 2...
Is that a fifth?
Yep!
Well... and those are my tricks

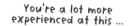

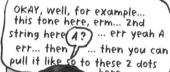

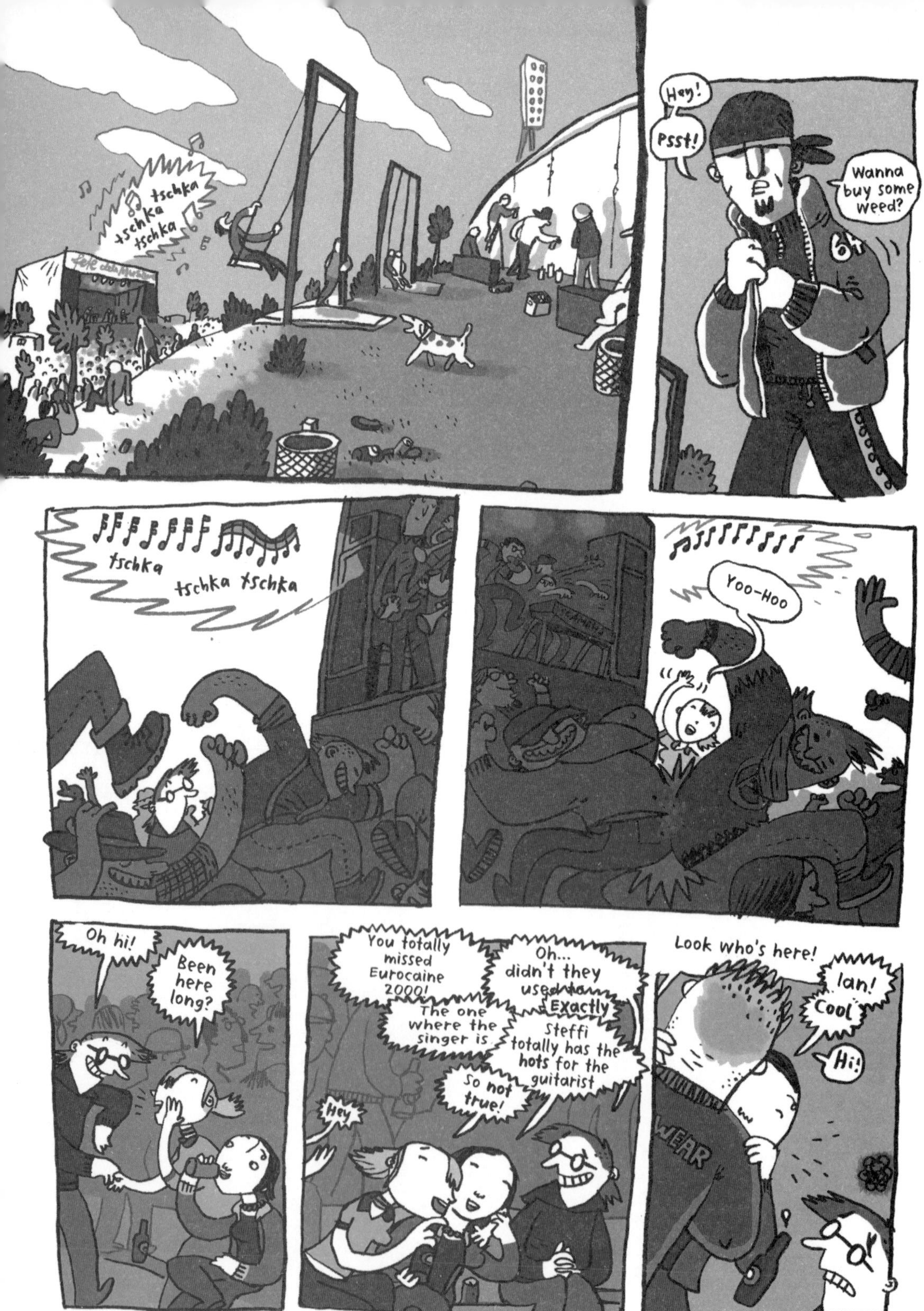

tschka
tschka
tschka
Hey!
Psst!
Wanna buy some weed?
tschka
tschka tschka
Yoo-Hoo
Oh hi!
Been here long?
You totally missed Eurocaine 2000!
Oh... didn't they used
The one where the singer is
Exactly
Steffi totally has the hots for the guitarist
So not true!
Hey
Look who's here!
Ian!
Cool
Hi!
WEAR

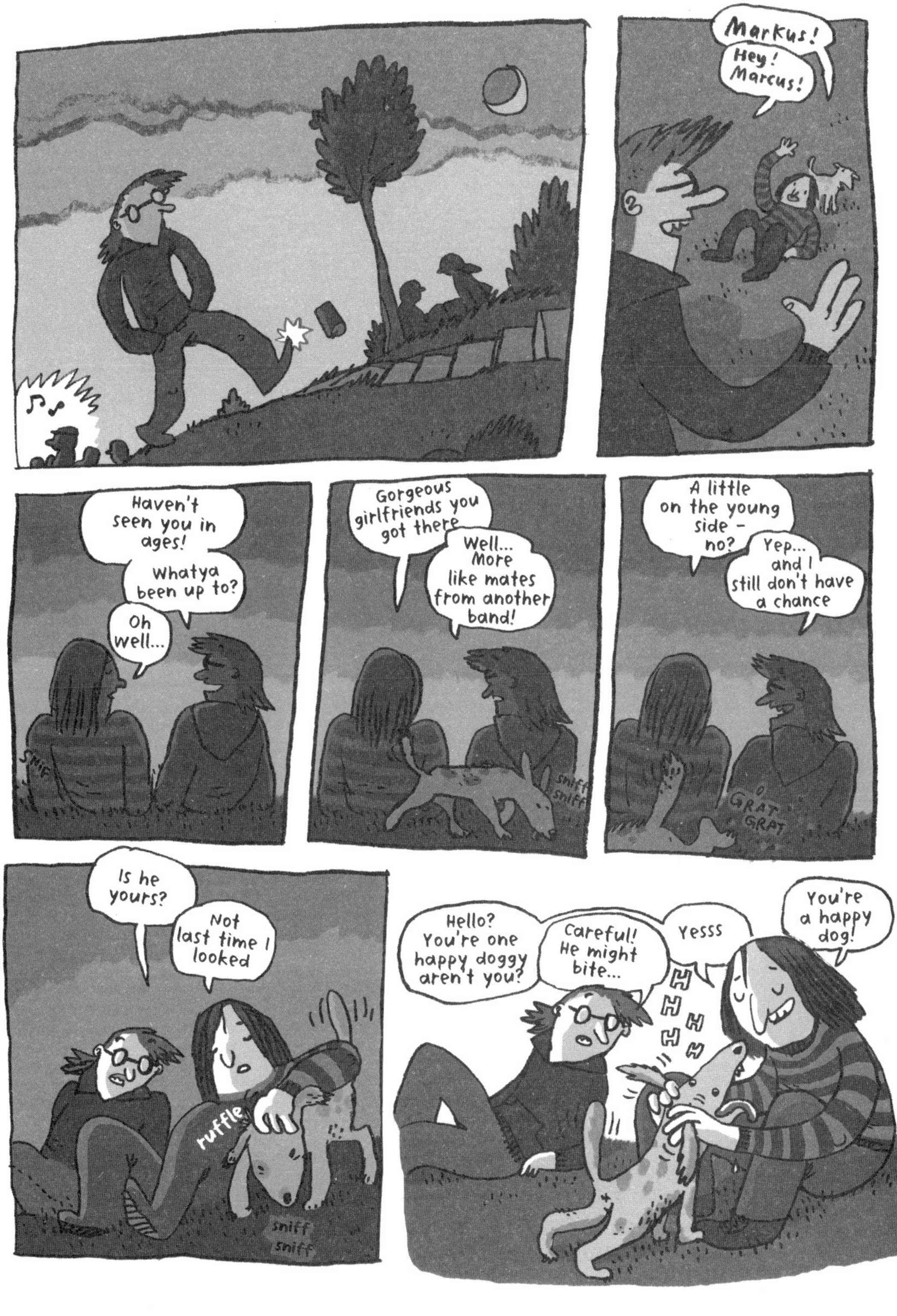
Markus!
Hey! Marcus!
Haven't seen you in ages!
Whatya been up to?
Oh well...
SNIF
Gorgeous girlfriends you got there
Well... More like mates from another band!
sniff sniff
A little on the young side - no?
Yep... and I still don't have a chance
GRAT GRAT
Is he yours?
Not last time I looked
ruffle
sniff sniff
Hello? You're one happy doggy aren't you?
Careful! He might bite...
Yesss
HHHHHH
You're a happy dog!

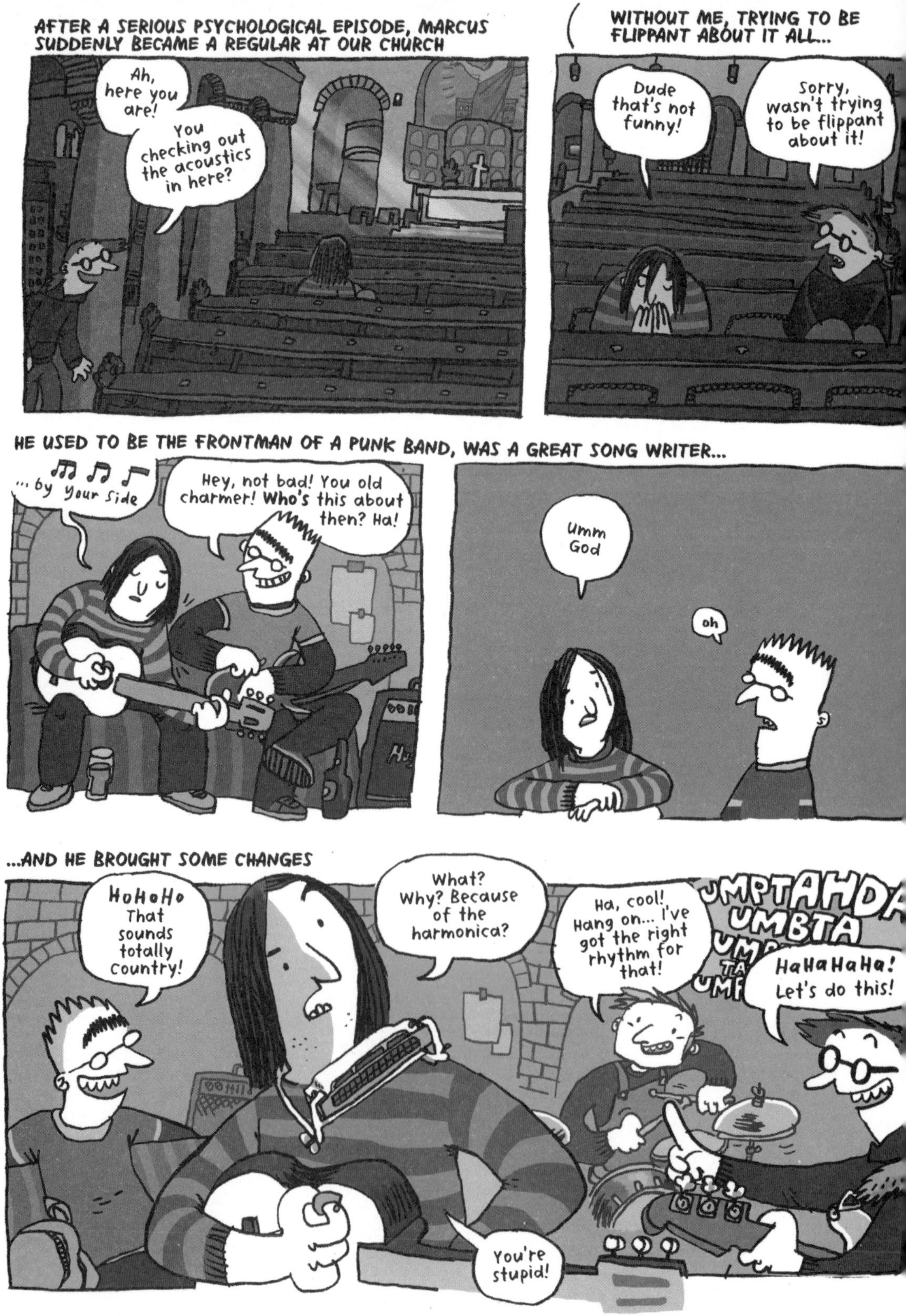
AFTER A SERIOUS PSYCHOLOGICAL EPISODE, MARCUS SUDDENLY BECAME A REGULAR AT OUR CHURCH
Ah, here you are!
You checking out the acoustics in here?
(WITHOUT ME, TRYING TO BE FLIPPANT ABOUT IT ALL...
Dude that's not funny!
Sorry, wasn't trying to be flippant about it!
HE USED TO BE THE FRONTMAN OF A PUNK BAND, WAS A GREAT SONG WRITER...
... by your side
Hey, not bad! You old charmer! Who's this about then? Ha!
Umm God
oh
...AND HE BROUGHT SOME CHANGES
HoHoHo That sounds totally country!
What? Why? Because of the harmonica?
Ha, cool! Hang on... I've got the right rhythm for that!
UMPTAHDA
UMBTA
HaHaHaHa! Let's do this!
You're stupid!

NOT JUST MUSICALLY

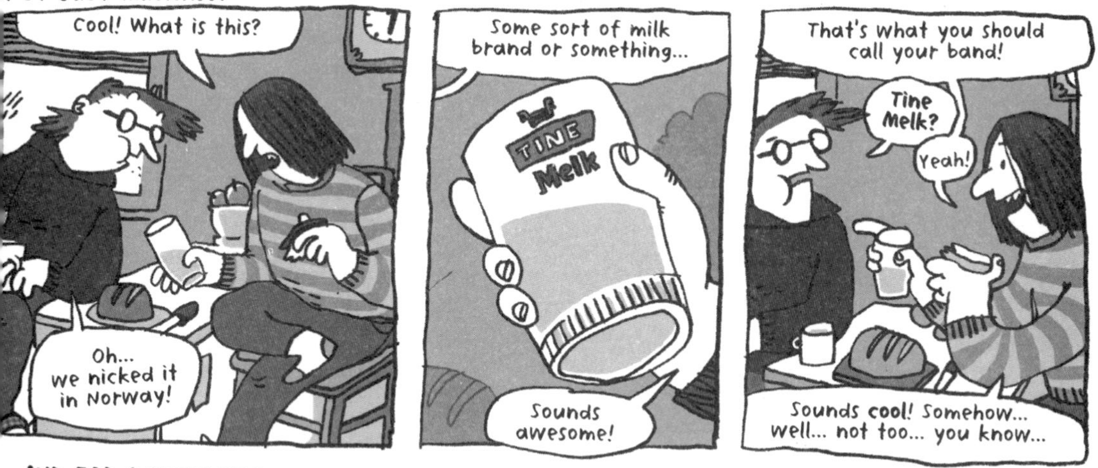
Cool! What is this?
Oh... we nicked it in Norway!
Some sort of milk brand or something...
TINE
Melk
Sounds awesome!
That's what you should call your band!
Tine Melk?
Yeah!
Sounds cool! Somehow... well... not too... you know...

AND FOR A SHORT WHILE WE EVEN HAD A SINGER AGAIN

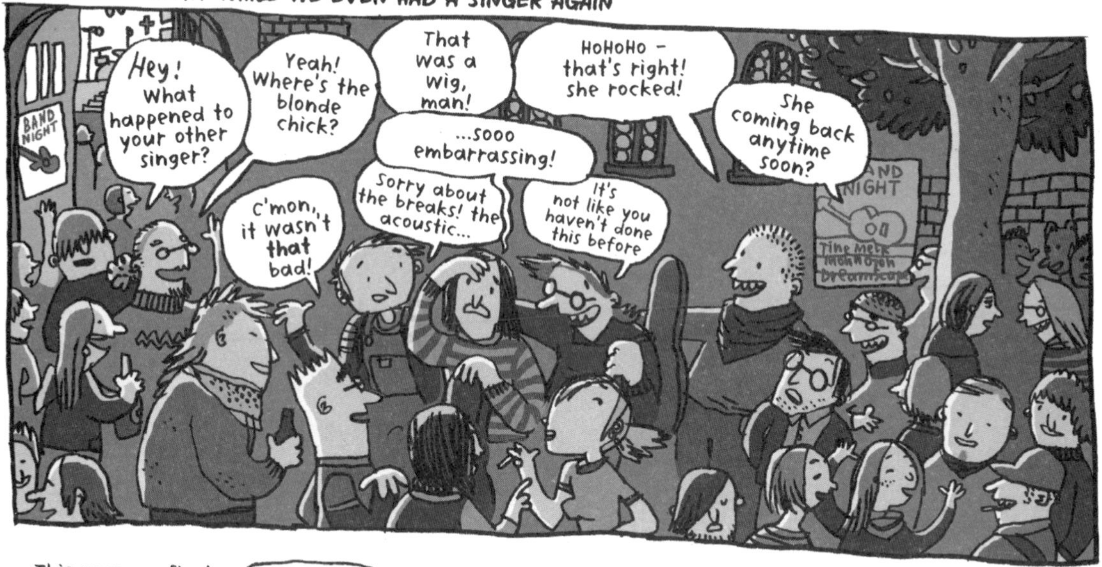
BAND NIGHT
Hey! What happened to your other singer?
Yeah! Where's the blonde chick?
That was a wig, man!
HoHoHo – that's right! she rocked!
She coming back anytime soon?
...sooo embarrassing!
C'mon, it wasn't that bad!
Sorry about the breaks! the acoustic...
It's not like you haven't done this before
Tine Melk

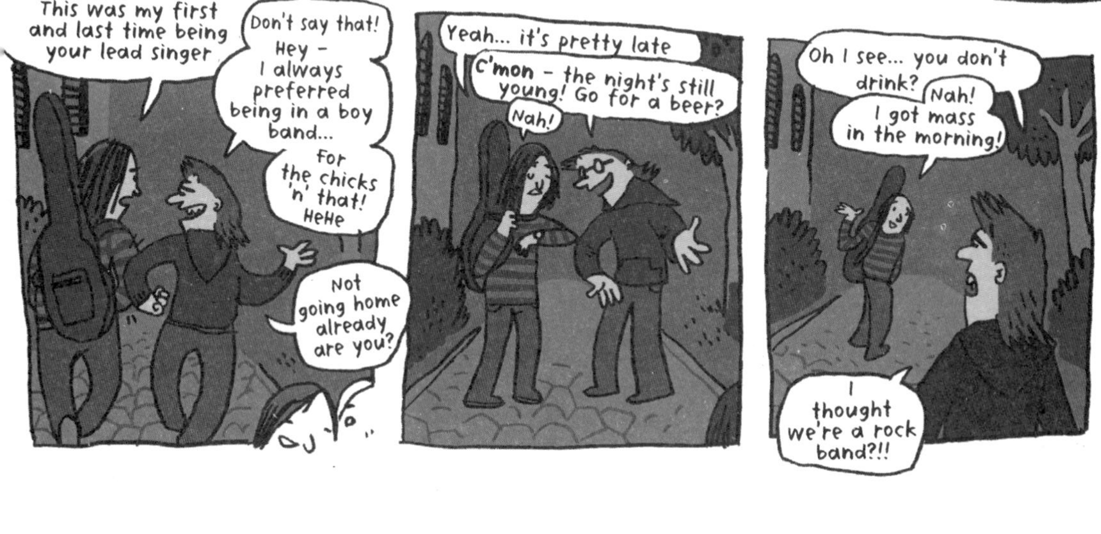
This was my first and last time being your lead singer
Don't say that! Hey – I always preferred being in a boy band...
For the chicks 'n' that! HeHe
Not going home already are you?
Yeah... it's pretty late
C'mon – the night's still young! Go for a beer?
Nah!
Oh I see... you don't drink?
Nah! I got mass in the morning!
I thought we're a rock band?!!

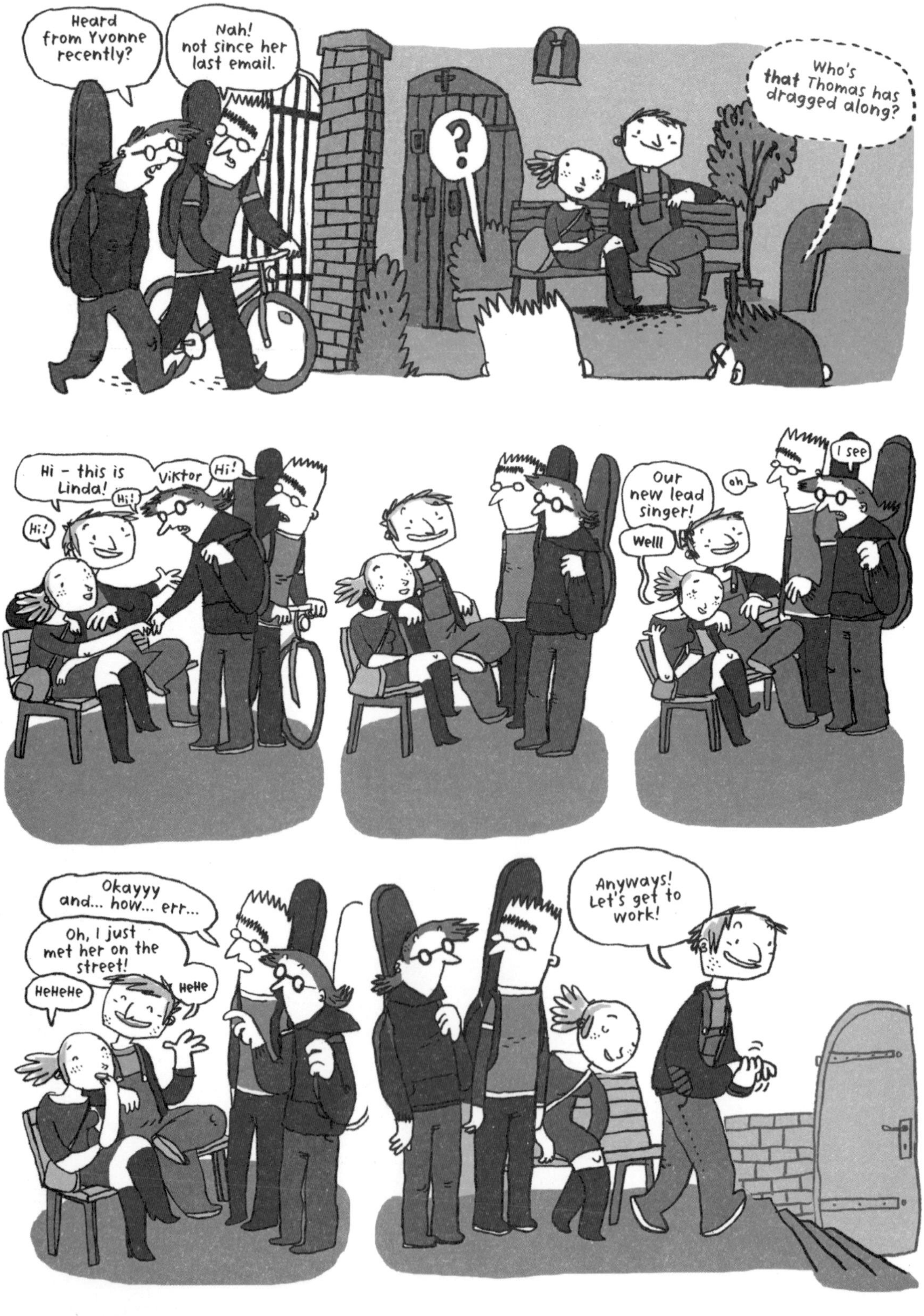
Heard from Yvonne recently?
Nah! not since her last email.
?
Who's that Thomas has dragged along?
Hi - this is Linda!
Hi!
Hi!
Viktor
Hi!
Our new lead singer!
Welll
oh
I see
Okayyy and... how... err...
Oh, I just met her on the street!
HeHeHe
HeHe
Anyways! Let's get to work!

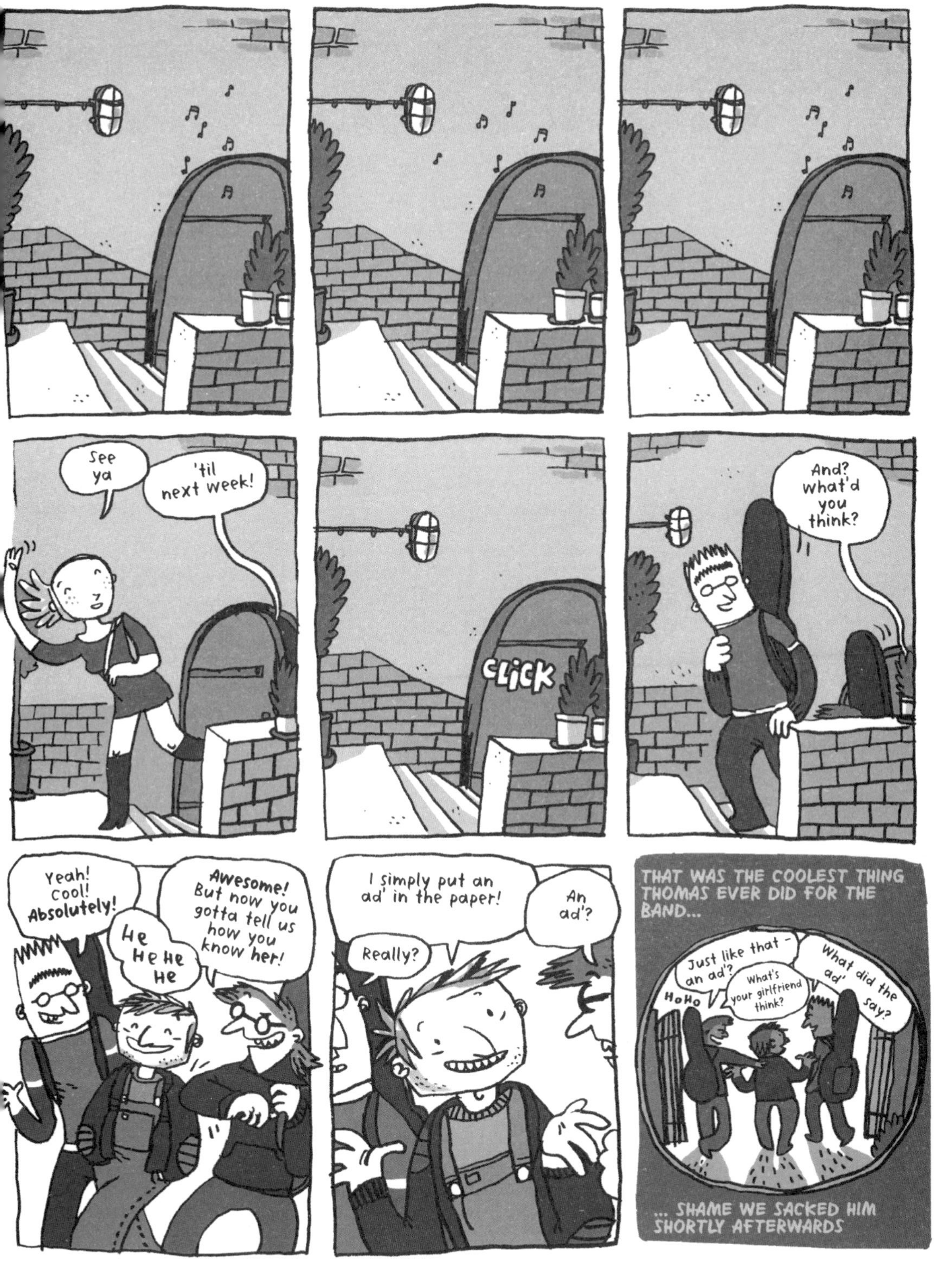
See ya
'til next week!
CLICK
And? what'd you think?
Yeah! Cool! Absolutely!
He He He He
Awesome! But now you gotta tell us how you know her!
I simply put an ad' in the paper!
Really?
An ad'?
THAT WAS THE COOLEST THING THOMAS EVER DID FOR THE BAND...
Just like that - an ad'?
HoHo
What's your girlfriend think?
What did the ad' say?
... SHAME WE SACKED HIM SHORTLY AFTERWARDS

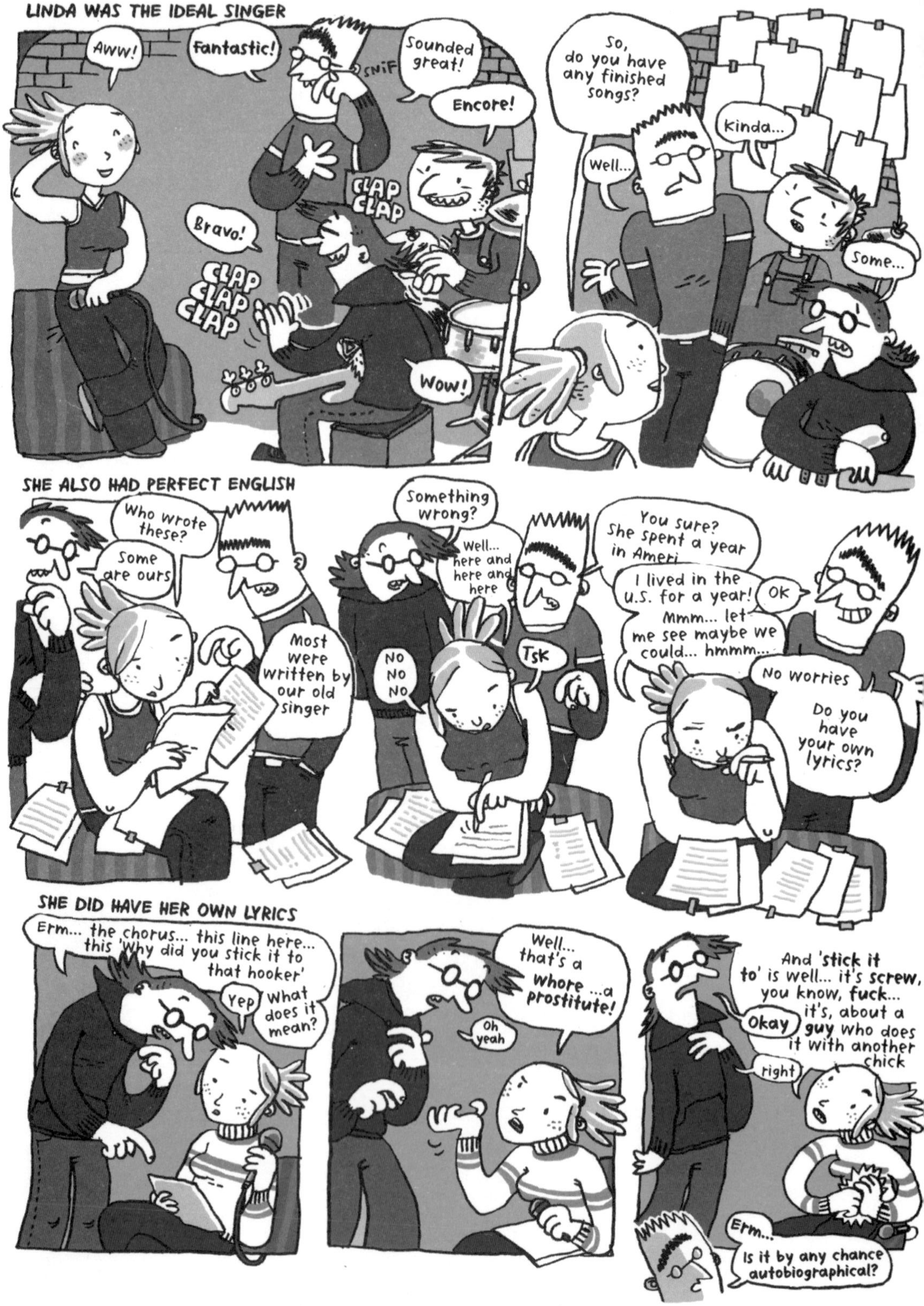
LINDA WAS THE IDEAL SINGER
Aww!
Fantastic!
Sounded great!
SNIF
Encore!
CLAP CLAP
Bravo!
CLAP CLAP CLAP
Wow!
So, do you have any finished songs?
Well...
Kinda...
Some...
SHE ALSO HAD PERFECT ENGLISH
Who wrote these?
Some are ours
Most were written by our old singer
Something wrong?
Well... here and here and here
NO NO NO
Tsk
You sure? She spent a year in Ameri
I lived in the U.S. for a year!
OK
Mmm... let me see maybe we could... hmmm...
No worries
Do you have your own lyrics?
SHE DID HAVE HER OWN LYRICS
Erm... the chorus... this line here... this 'Why did you stick it to that hooker'
Yep
What does it mean?
Well... that's a whore ...a prostitute!
Oh yeah
And 'stick it to' is well... it's screw, you know, fuck... it's, about a guy who does it with another chick
Okay
right
Erm...
Is it by any chance autobiographical?

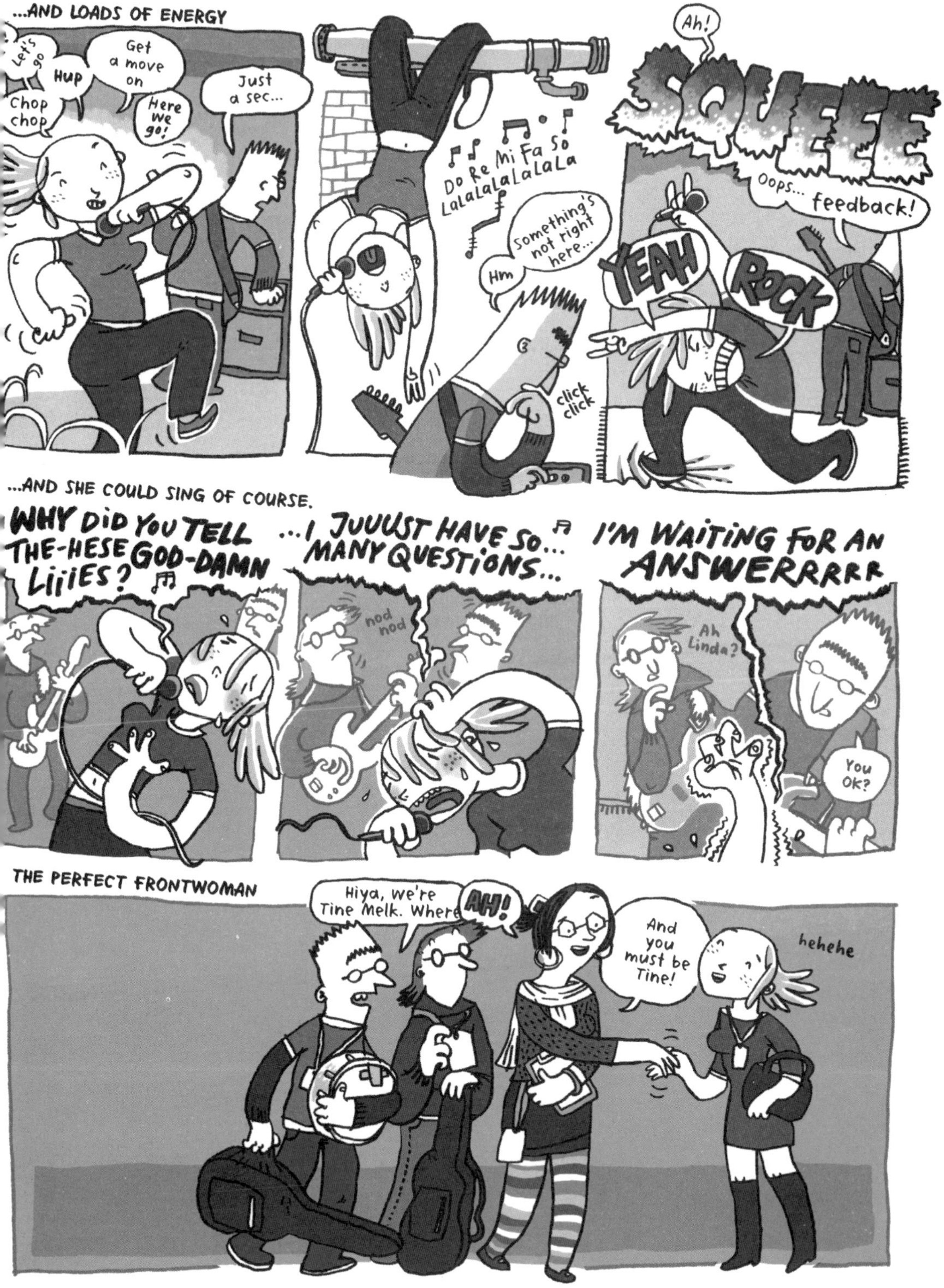

...AND LOADS OF ENERGY
Let's go
Hup
Get a move on
Chop chop
Here we go!
Just a sec...
Do Re Mi Fa So LaLaLaLaLaLaLa
Something's not right here...
Hm
click click
Ah!
SQUEEE
Oops... feedback!
YEAH
ROCK
...AND SHE COULD SING OF COURSE.
WHY DID YOU TELL THE-HESE GOD-DAMN LIiiES?
...I JUUUST HAVE SO... MANY QUESTIONS...
nod nod
I'M WAITING FOR AN ANSWERRRRR
Ah Linda?
You OK?
THE PERFECT FRONTWOMAN
Hiya, we're Tine Melk. Where
AH!
And you must be Tine!
hehehe

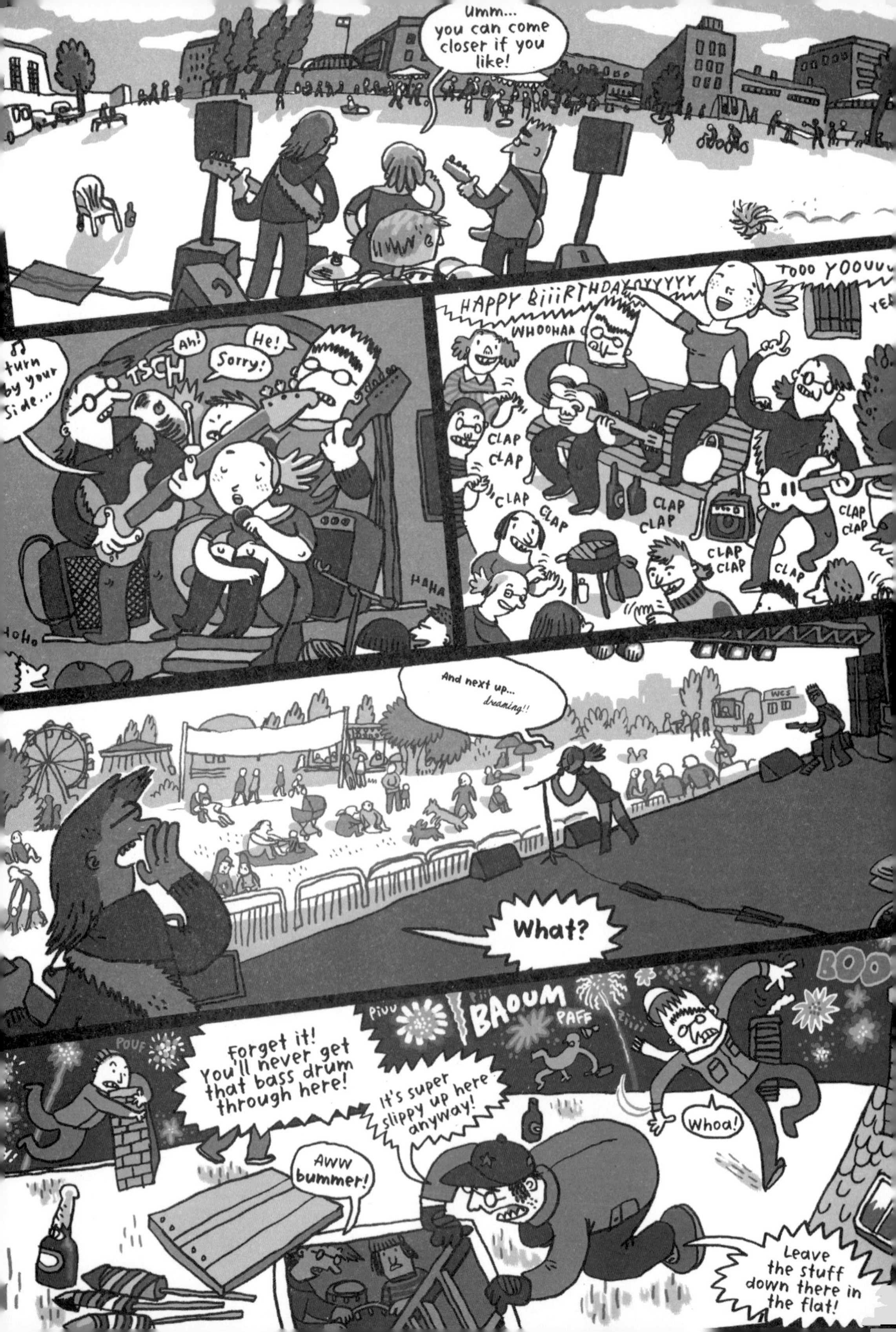
umm... you can come closer if you like!
♫ turn by your side...
TSCH
Ah!
Sorry!
He!
HAHA
HOHO
HAPPY BiiiRTHDAYYYYY
TOOO YOOUUU
WHOOHAA
CLAP CLAP
CLAP
CLAP
CLAP CLAP
CLAP CLAP
CLAP CLAP
CLAP
And next up... dreaming!!
What?
PIUU
BAOUM
PAFF
POUF
Forget it! You'll never get that bass drum through here!
It's super slippy up here anyway!
Whoa!
AWW bummer!
Leave the stuff down there in the flat!

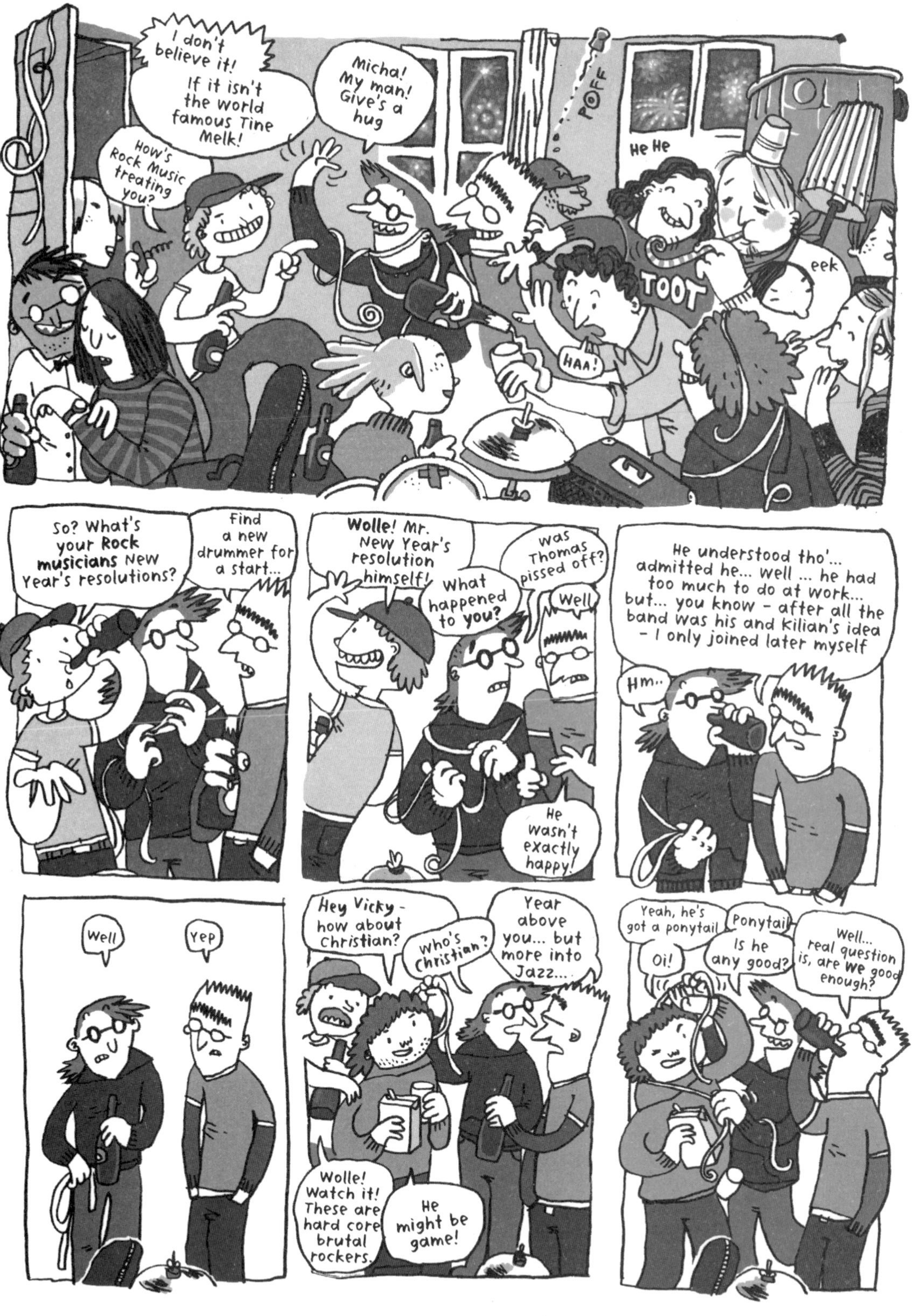
I don't believe it! If it isn't the world famous Tine Melk!
How's Rock Music treating you?
Micha! My man! Give's a hug
POFF
He He
TOOT
eek
HAA!
So? What's your Rock musicians New Year's resolutions?
Find a new drummer for a start...
Wolle! Mr. New Year's resolution himself!
What happened to you?
Was Thomas pissed off?
Well
He wasn't exactly happy!
He understood tho'... admitted he... well ... he had too much to do at work... but... you know - after all the band was his and Kilian's idea - I only joined later myself
Hm..
Well
Yep
Hey Vicky - how about Christian?
Who's Christian?
Year above you... but more into Jazz...
Wolle! Watch it! These are hard core brutal rockers.
He might be game!
Yeah, he's got a ponytail
Ponytail
Oi!
Is he any good?
Well... real question is, are we good enough?

CHRISTIAN WAS A PROFESSIONAL

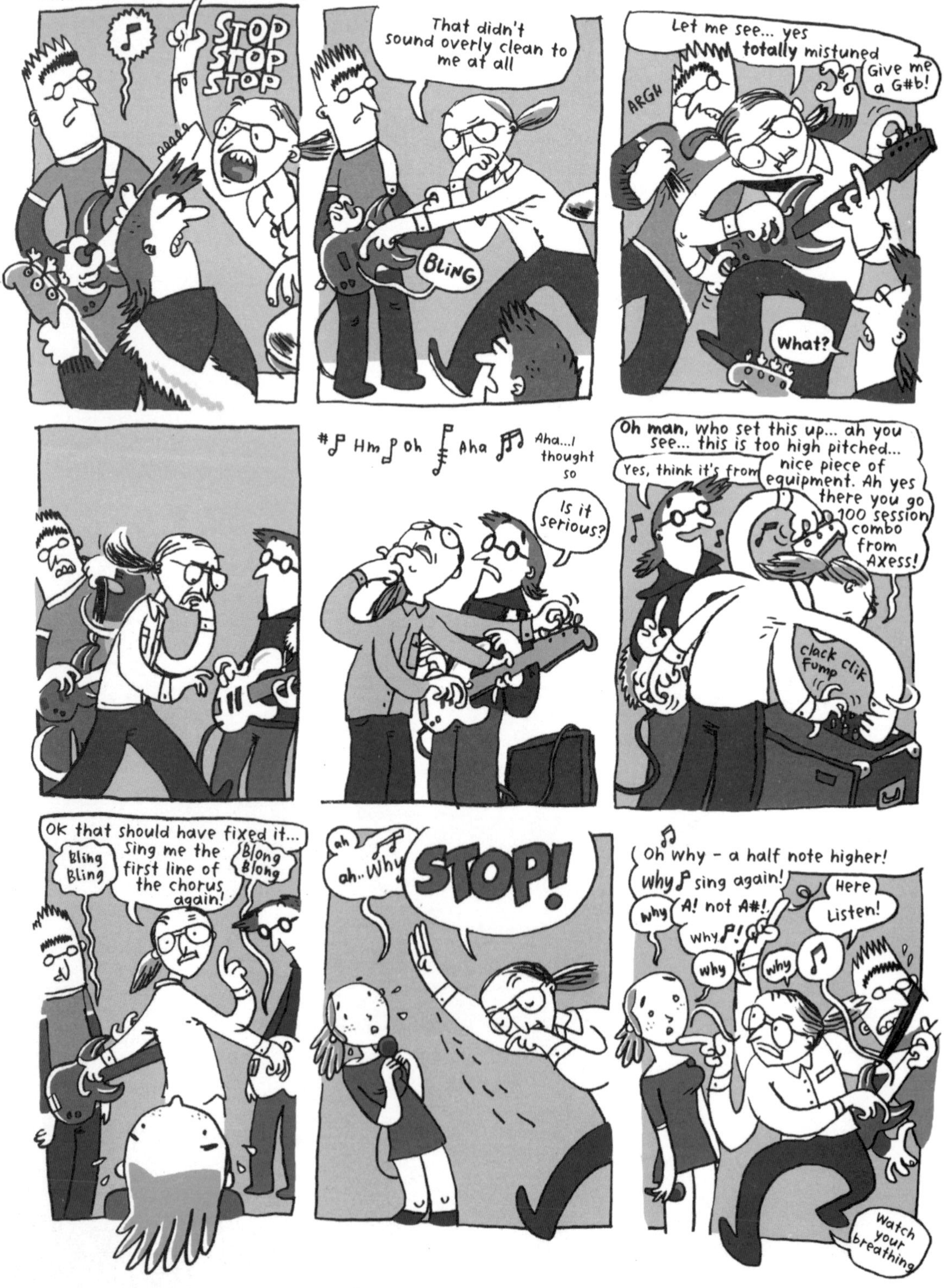

STOP STOP STOP
That didn't sound overly clean to me at all
BLING
Let me see... yes totally mistuned
ARGH
Give me a G#b!
What?
Hm Oh Aha
Aha...I thought so
Is it serious?
Oh man, who set this up... ah you see... this is too high pitched...
Yes, think it's from
nice piece of equipment. Ah yes there you go 100 session combo from Axess!
clack clik Fump
Ok that should have fixed it...
Bling Bling
Sing me the first line of the chorus again!
Blong Blong
ah
ah.. Why
STOP!
Oh why - a half note higher!
Why sing again!
Why
A! not A#!
Why
Here Listen!
Why
Why
Watch your breathing

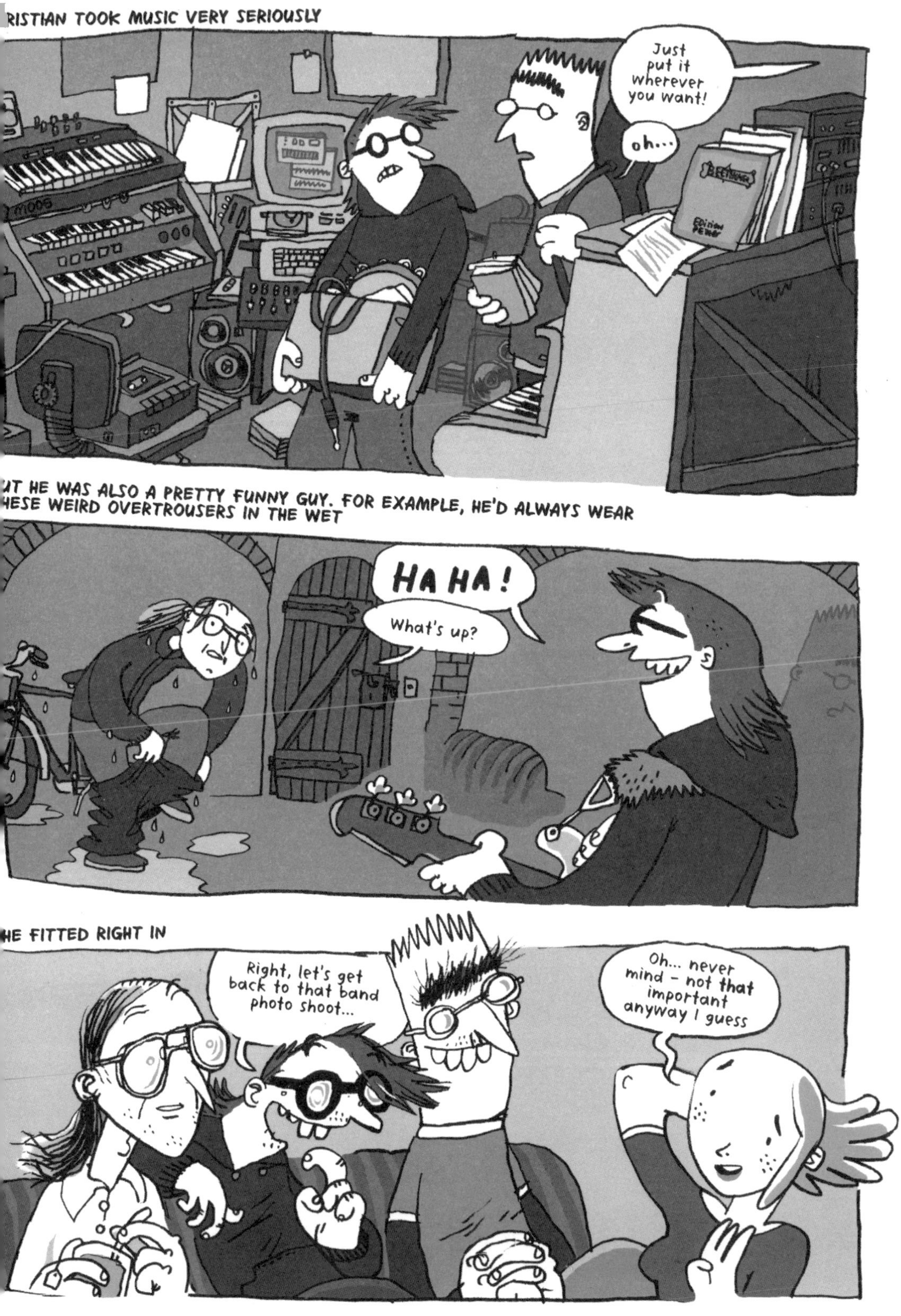
RISTIAN TOOK MUSIC VERY SERIOUSLY
Just put it wherever you want!
oh...
UT HE WAS ALSO A PRETTY FUNNY GUY. FOR EXAMPLE, HE'D ALWAYS WEAR
HESE WEIRD OVERTROUSERS IN THE WET
HA HA!
What's up?
HE FITTED RIGHT IN
Right, let's get back to that band photo shoot...
Oh... never mind - not that important anyway I guess

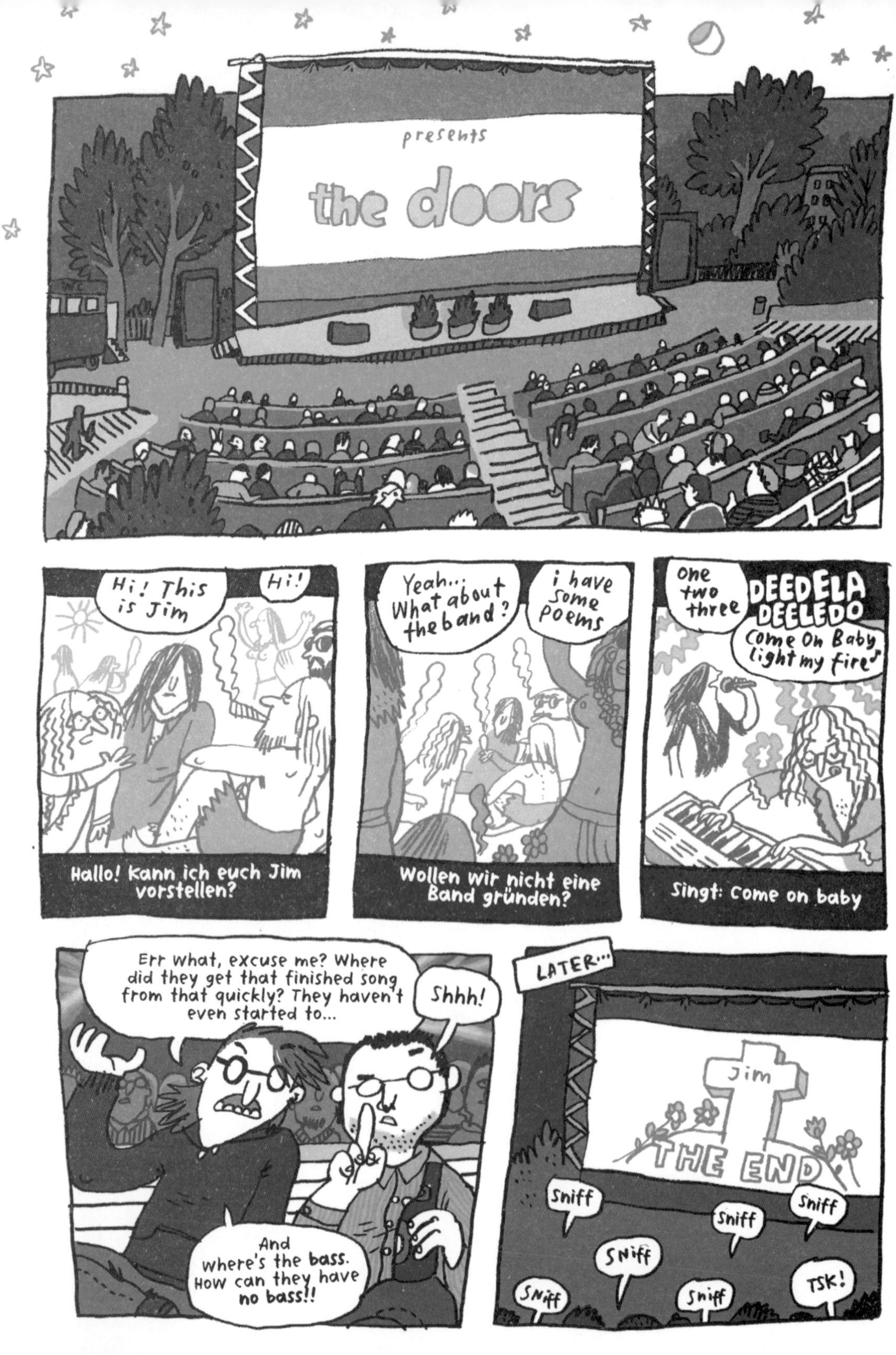
presents
the doors
Hi! This is Jim
Hi!
Hallo! Kann ich euch Jim vorstellen?
Yeah... What about the band?
i have some poems
Wollen wir nicht eine Band gründen?
One two three
DEEDELA DEELEDO
Come On Baby light my fire
Singt: Come on baby
Err what, excuse me? Where did they get that finished song from that quickly? They haven't even started to...
Shhh!
And where's the bass. How can they have no bass!!
LATER...
Jim
THE END
Sniff
Sniff
Sniff
SNiff
SNiff
Sniff
TSK!

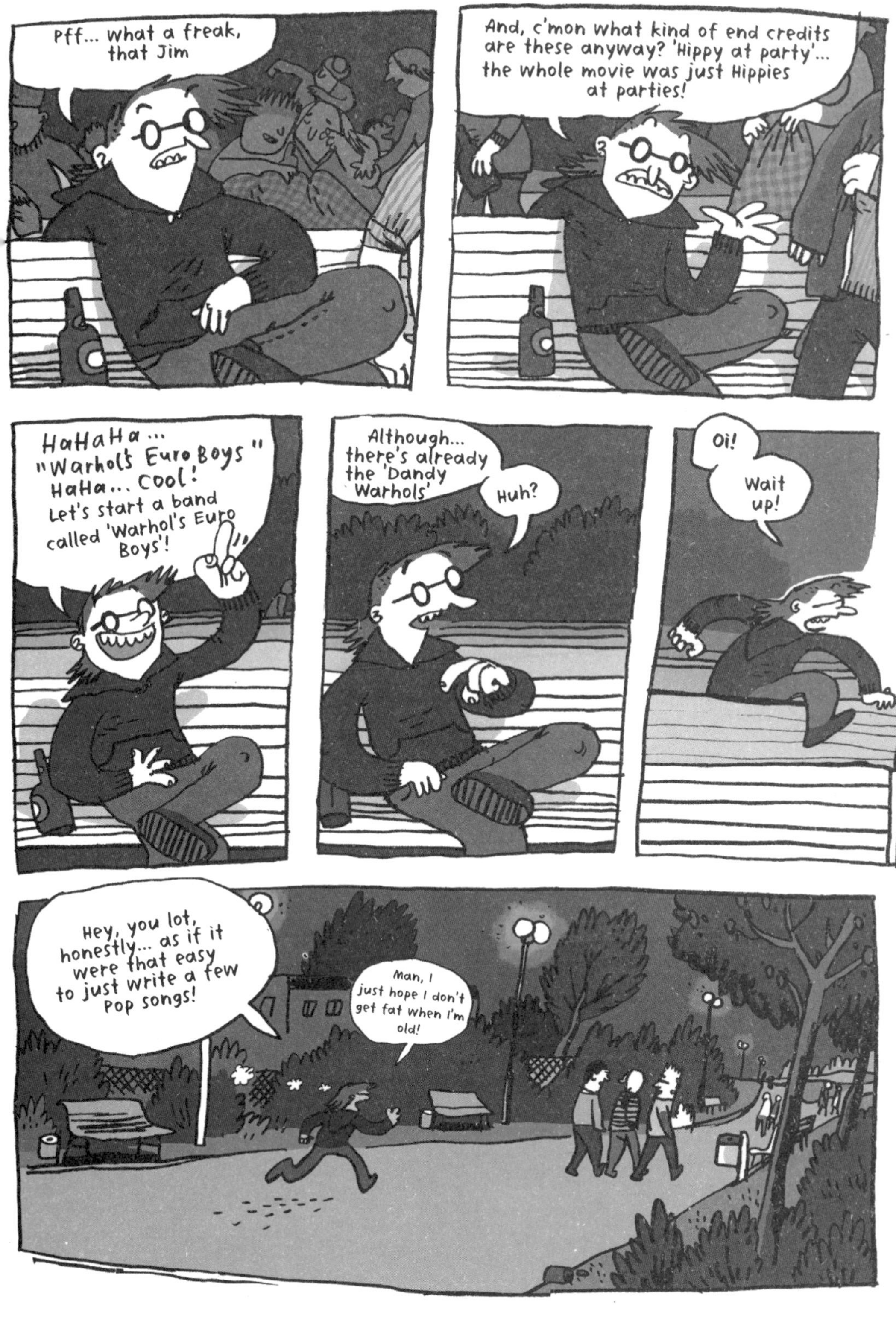
Pff... what a freak, that Jim
And, c'mon what kind of end credits are these anyway? 'Hippy at party'... the whole movie was just Hippies at parties!
HaHaHa... "Warhol's Euro Boys" HaHa... cool! Let's start a band called 'Warhol's Euro Boys'!
Although... there's already the 'Dandy Warhols'
Huh?
Oi!
Wait up!
Hey, you lot, honestly... as if it were that easy to just write a few Pop songs!
Man, I just hope I don't get fat when I'm old!

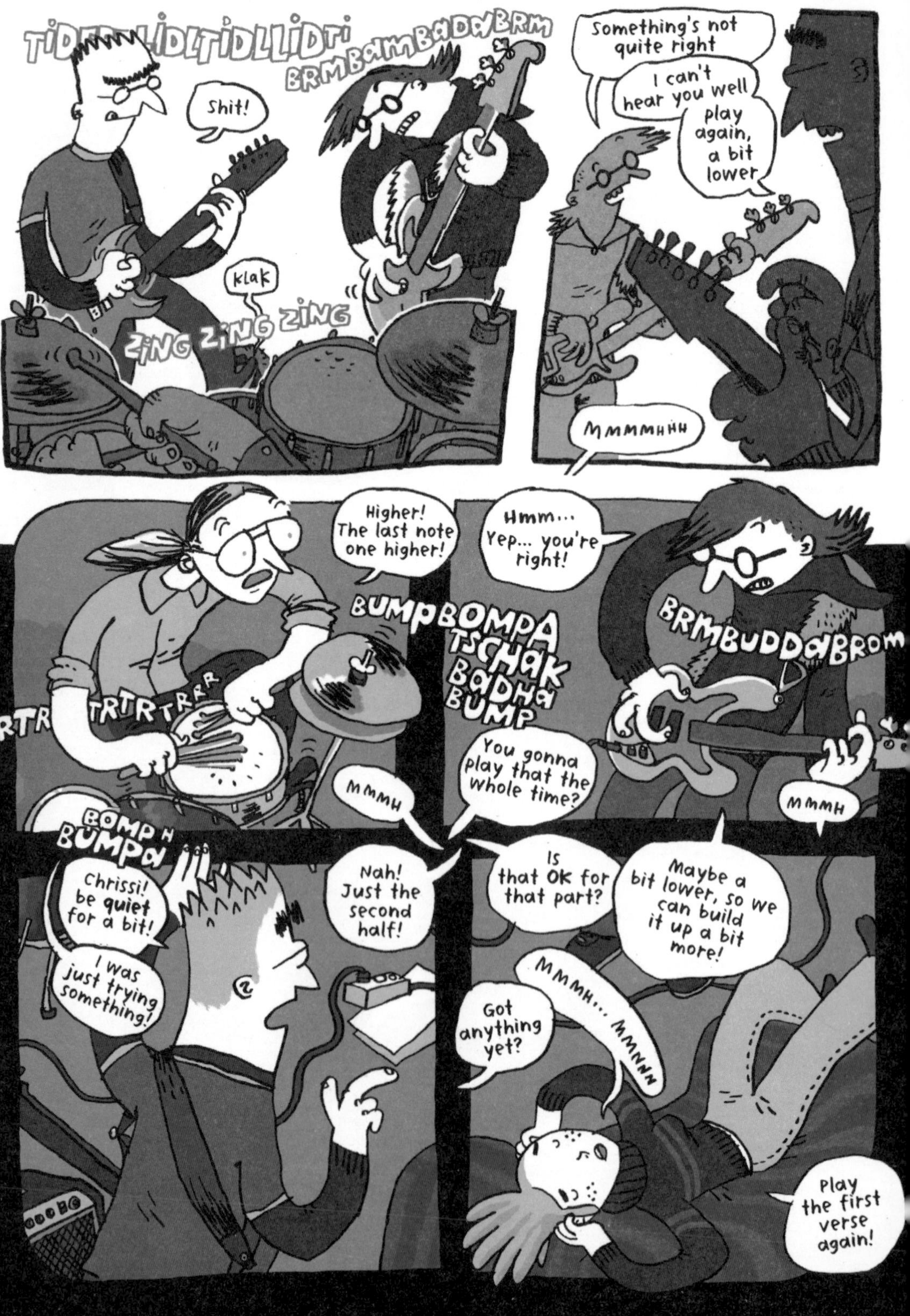

BRMBamBaDaBRM
Shit!
klak
ZiNG ZiNG ZiNG
Something's not quite right
I can't hear you well
play again, a bit lower
MMMMHHH
Higher! The last note one higher!
Hmm... Yep... you're right!
BUMPBOMPA TSCHAK BaDHa BUMP
RTR TRTRTRRR
BRMBUDDaBROM
You gonna play that the whole time?
MMMH
MMMH
BOMPH BUMPa
Chrissi! be quiet for a bit!
I was just trying something!
Nah! Just the second half!
Is that OK for that part?
Maybe a bit lower, so we can build it up a bit more!
MMMH... MMNN
Got anything yet?
Play the first verse again!

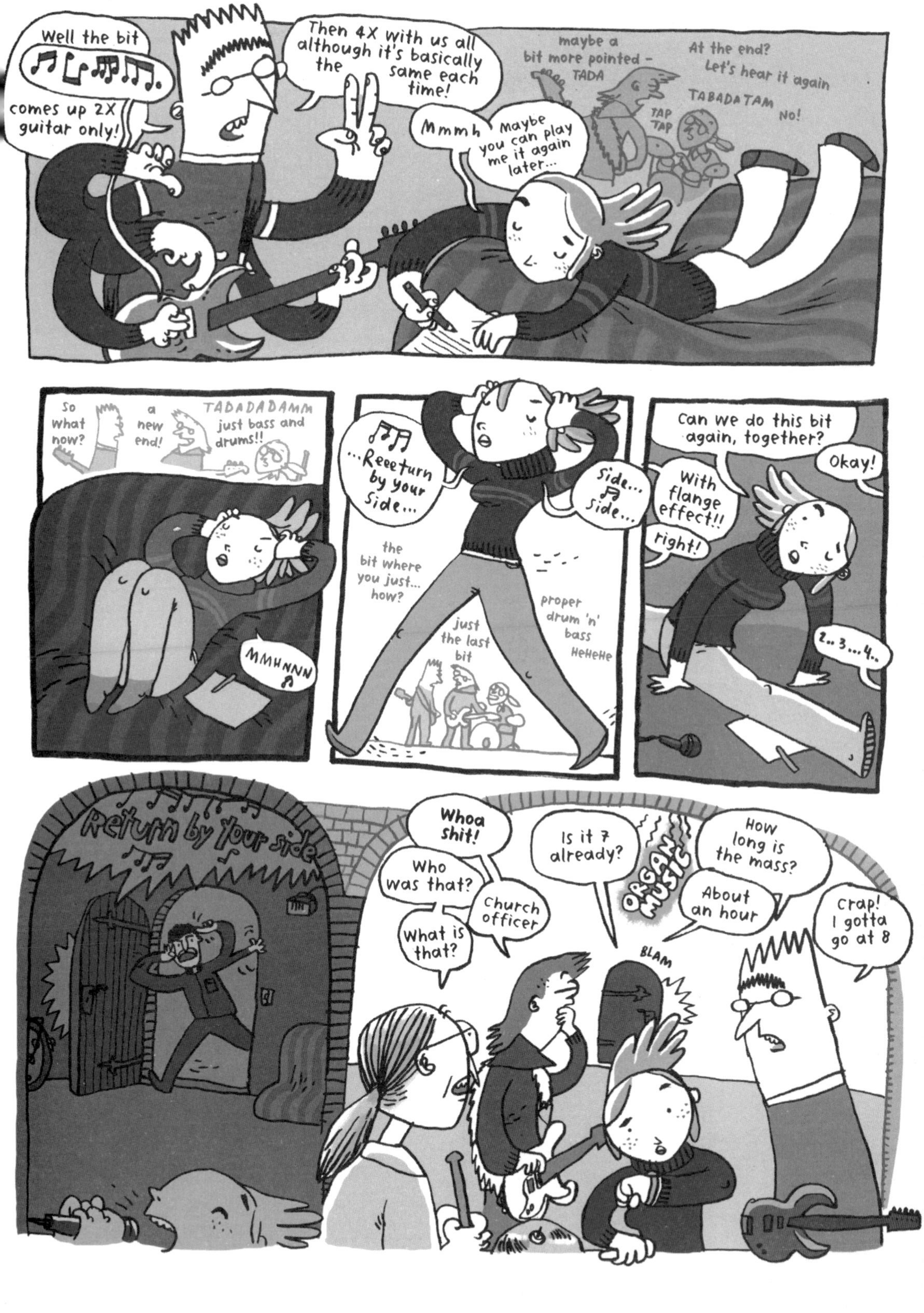

Well the bit
comes up 2X guitar only!
Then 4X with us all although it's basically the same each time!
maybe a bit more pointed - TADA
At the end?
Let's hear it again
TABADATAM
TAP TAP
NO!
Mmmh
Maybe you can play me it again later...
So what now?
a new end!
TADADADAMM
just bass and drums!!
MMHNNN
...Reeeturn by your Side...
Side... Side...
the bit where you just... how?
just the last bit
proper drum 'n' bass
HEHEHE
Can we do this bit again, together?
Okay!
With flange effect!!
right!
2.. 3... 4..
Return by your side
Whoa shit!
Who was that?
Church officer
What is that?
Is it 7 already?
ORGAN MUSIC
How long is the mass?
About an hour
BLAM
Crap! I gotta go at 8

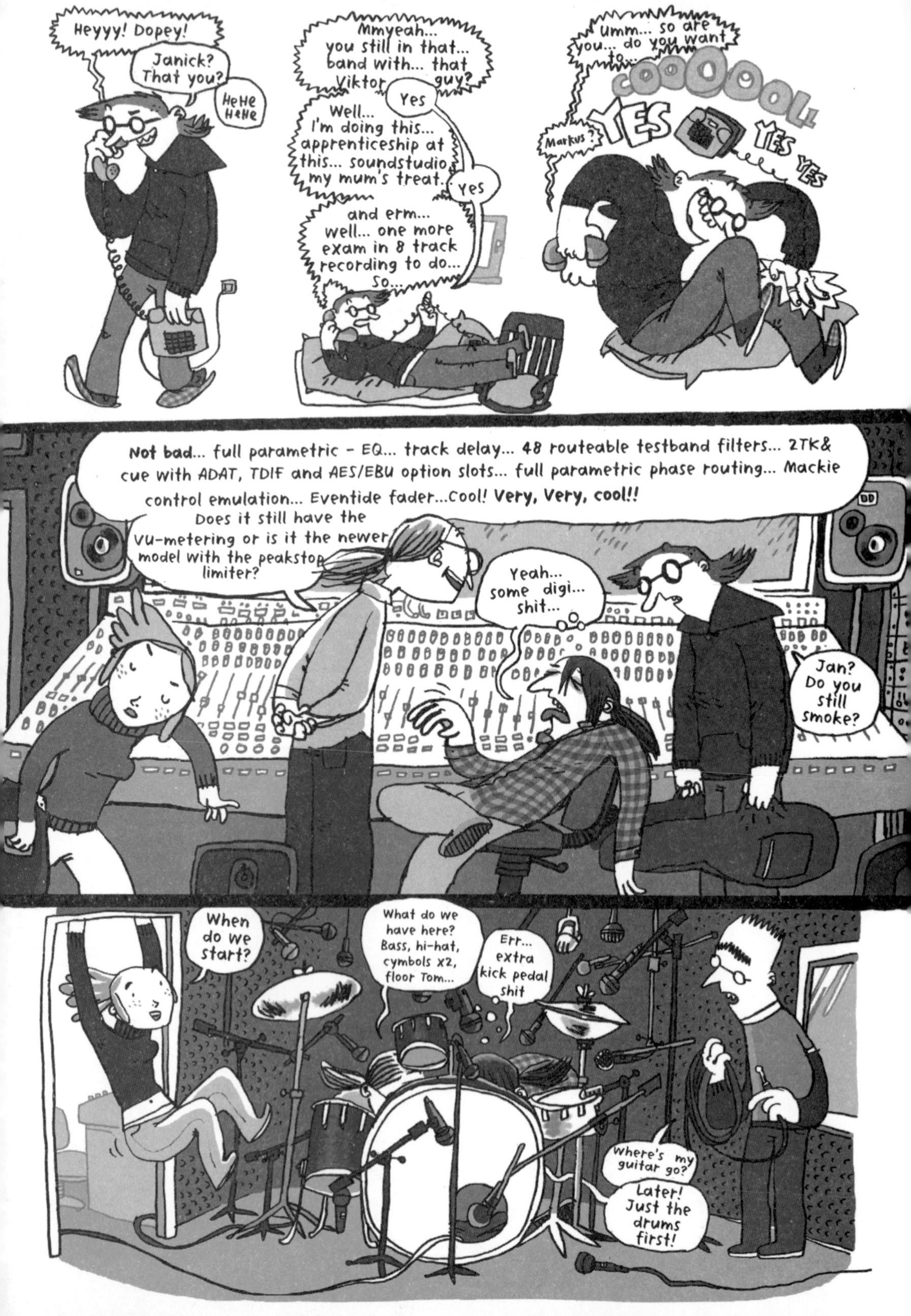
Heyyy! Dopey!
Janick? That you?
HeHe HeHe
Mmyeah... you still in that... band with... that Viktor guy?
Yes
Well... I'm doing this... apprenticeship at this... soundstudio my mum's treat...
Yes
and erm... well... one more exam in 8 track recording to do... So...
Umm... so are you... do you want to...
COOOOOOL
Markus?
YES
YES
YES
Not bad... full parametric - EQ... track delay... 48 routeable testband filters... 2TK& cue with ADAT, TDIF and AES/EBU option slots... full parametric phase routing... Mackie control emulation... Eventide fader...Cool! Very, Very, cool!!
Does it still have the VU-metering or is it the newer model with the peakstop limiter?
Yeah... some digi... shit...
Jan? Do you still smoke?
When do we start?
What do we have here? Bass, hi-hat, cymbols x2, floor Tom...
Err... extra kick pedal shit
Where's my guitar go?
Later! Just the drums first!

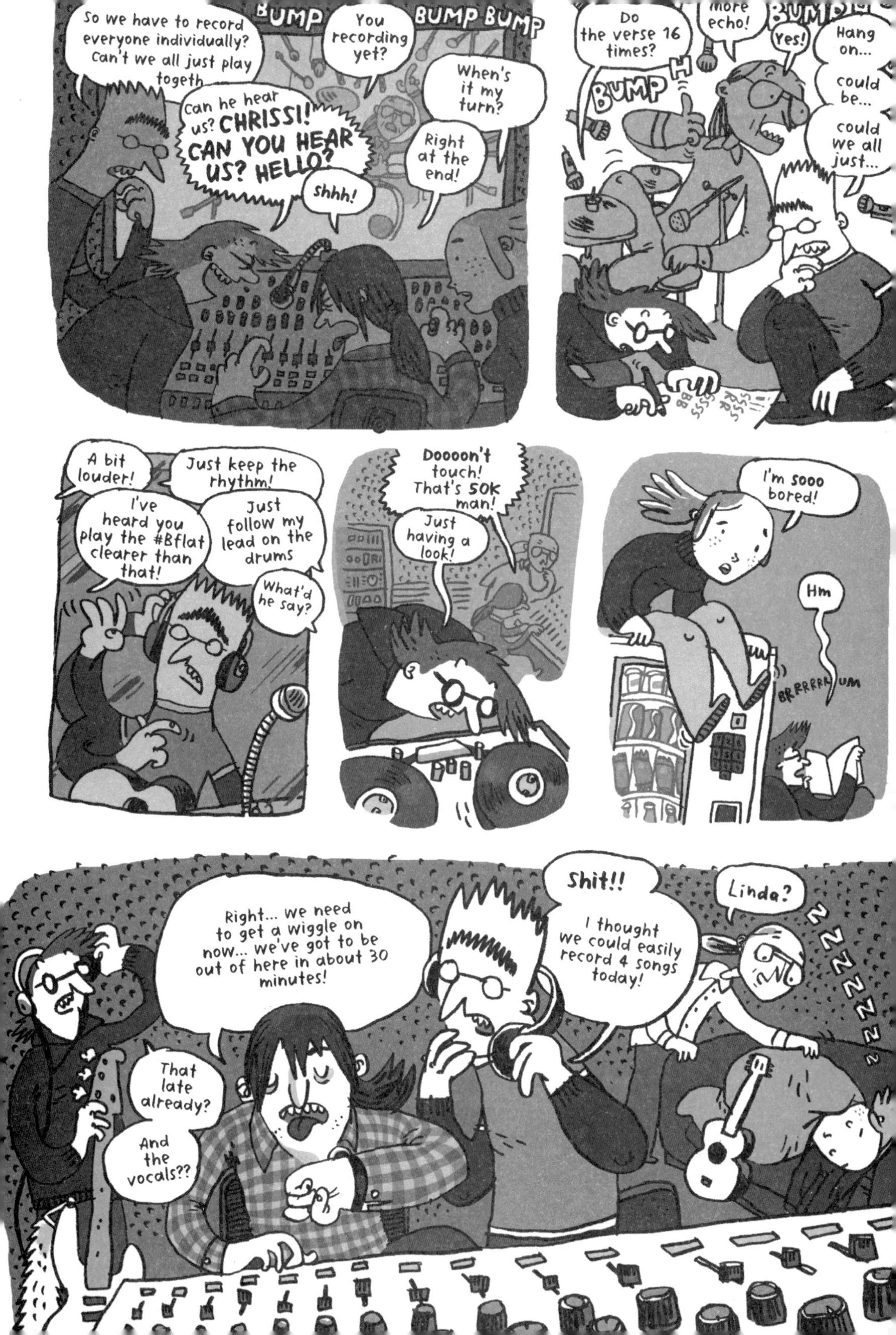

So we have to record everyone individually? Can't we all just play togeth
BUMP
You recording yet?
BUMP BUMP
Can he hear us? CHRISSI! CAN YOU HEAR US? HELLO?
When's it my turn?
Right at the end!
shhh!
Do the verse 16 times?
more echo!
Yes!
Hang on...
could be...
could we all just...
BUMPH
A bit louder!
Just keep the rhythm!
I've heard you play the #Bflat clearer than that!
Just follow my lead on the drums
What'd he say?
Doooon't touch! That's 50K man!
Just having a look!
I'm sooo bored!
Hm
BRRRRRRUM
Right... we need to get a wiggle on now... we've got to be out of here in about 30 minutes!
Shit!!
I thought we could easily record 4 songs today!
Linda?
That late already?
And the vocals??

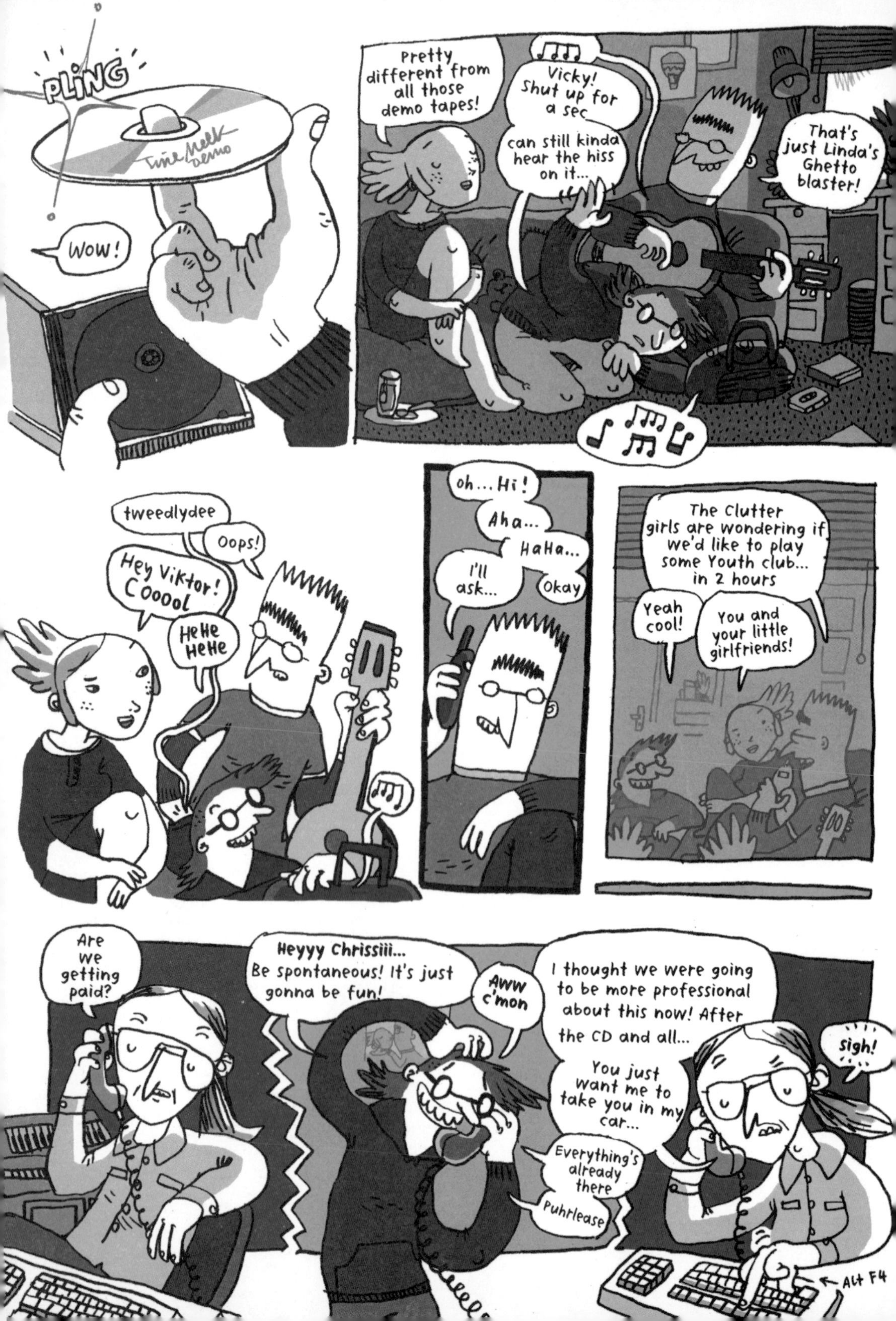
PLING
Tine Melk demo
WOW!
Pretty different from all those demo tapes!
Vicky! Shut up for a sec
can still kinda hear the hiss on it...
That's just Linda's Ghetto blaster!
tweedlydee
Oops!
Hey Viktor! Cooool
HeHe HeHe
oh... Hi!
Aha...
HaHa...
I'll ask...
Okay
The Clutter girls are wondering if we'd like to play some Youth club... in 2 hours
Yeah cool!
You and your little girlfriends!
Are we getting paid?
Heyyy Chrissiii...
Be spontaneous! It's just gonna be fun!
Aww c'mon
I thought we were going to be more professional about this now! After the CD and all...
You just want me to take you in my car...
Everything's already there
Puhrlease
Sigh!
Alt F4

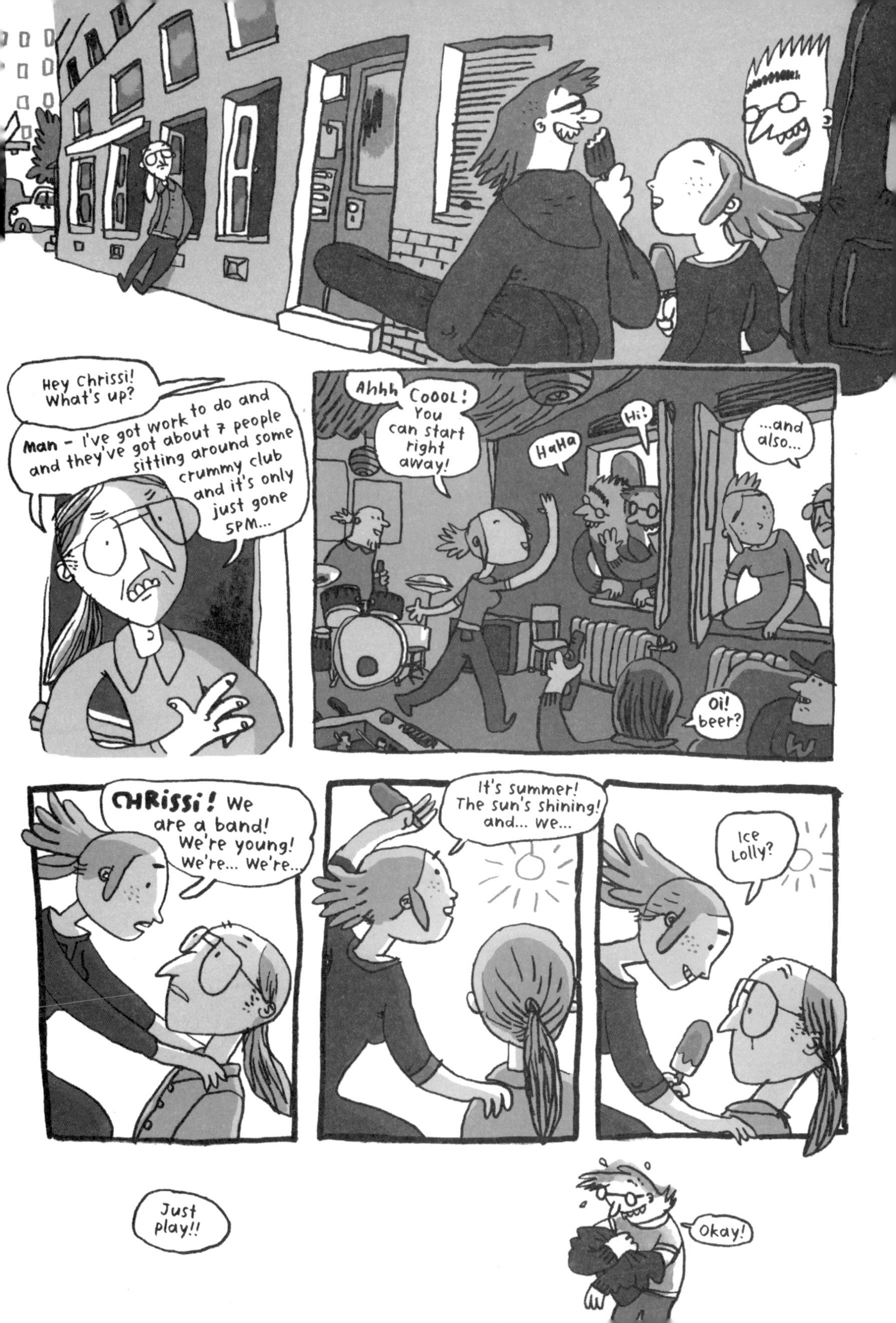

Hey Chrissi! What's up?
Man - I've got work to do and and they've got about 7 people sitting around some crummy club and it's only just gone 5PM...
Ahhh
COOOL! You can start right away!
HaHa
Hi!
...and also...
Oi! beer?
CHRISSI! We are a band! We're young! We're... We're...
It's summer! The sun's shining! and... we...
Ice Lolly?
Just play!!
Okay!

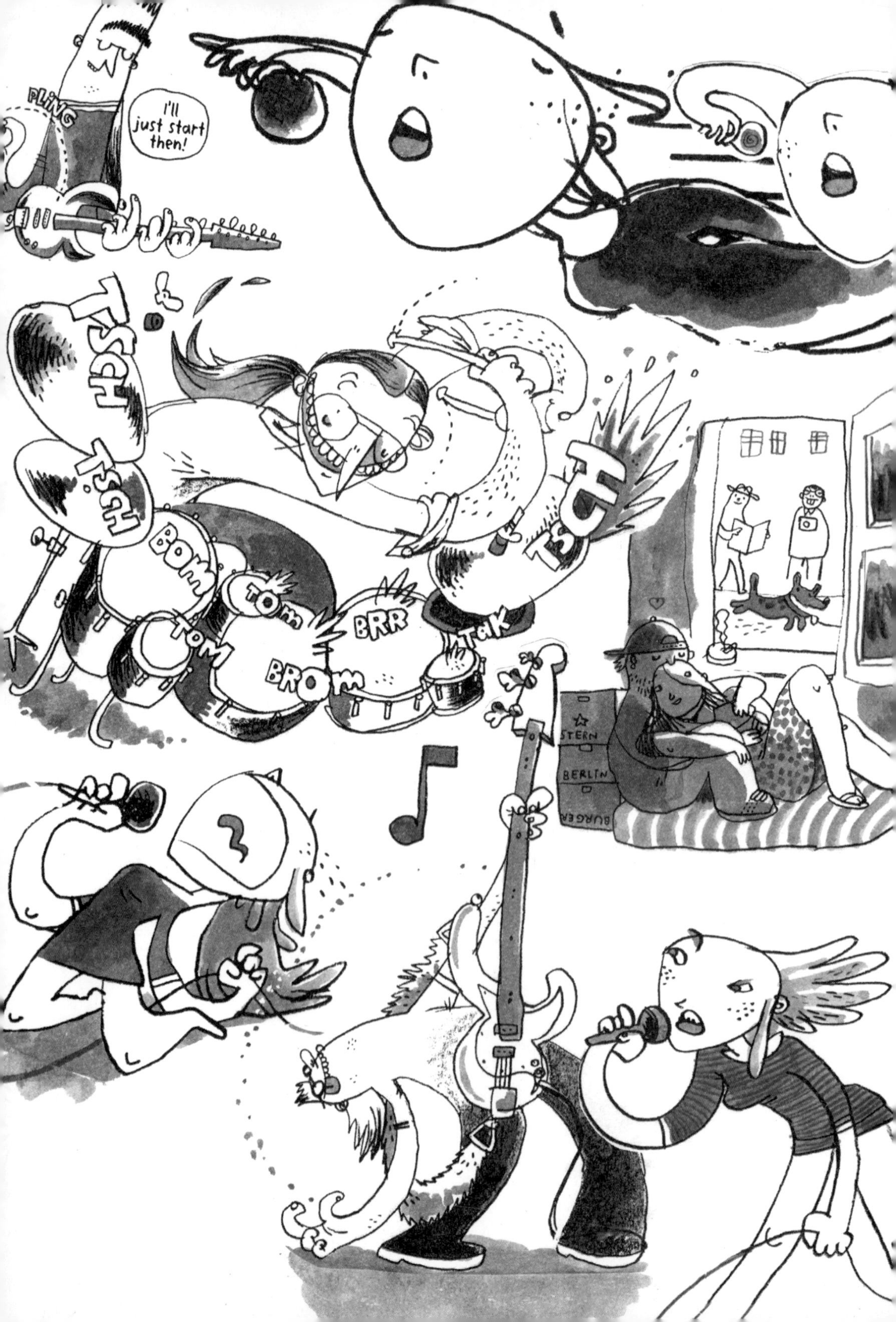

PLING
I'll just start then!
TSCH
TSCH
TSCH
BOM
TOM
TOM
BRR
BROM
TaK
STERN
BERLIN
BURGER

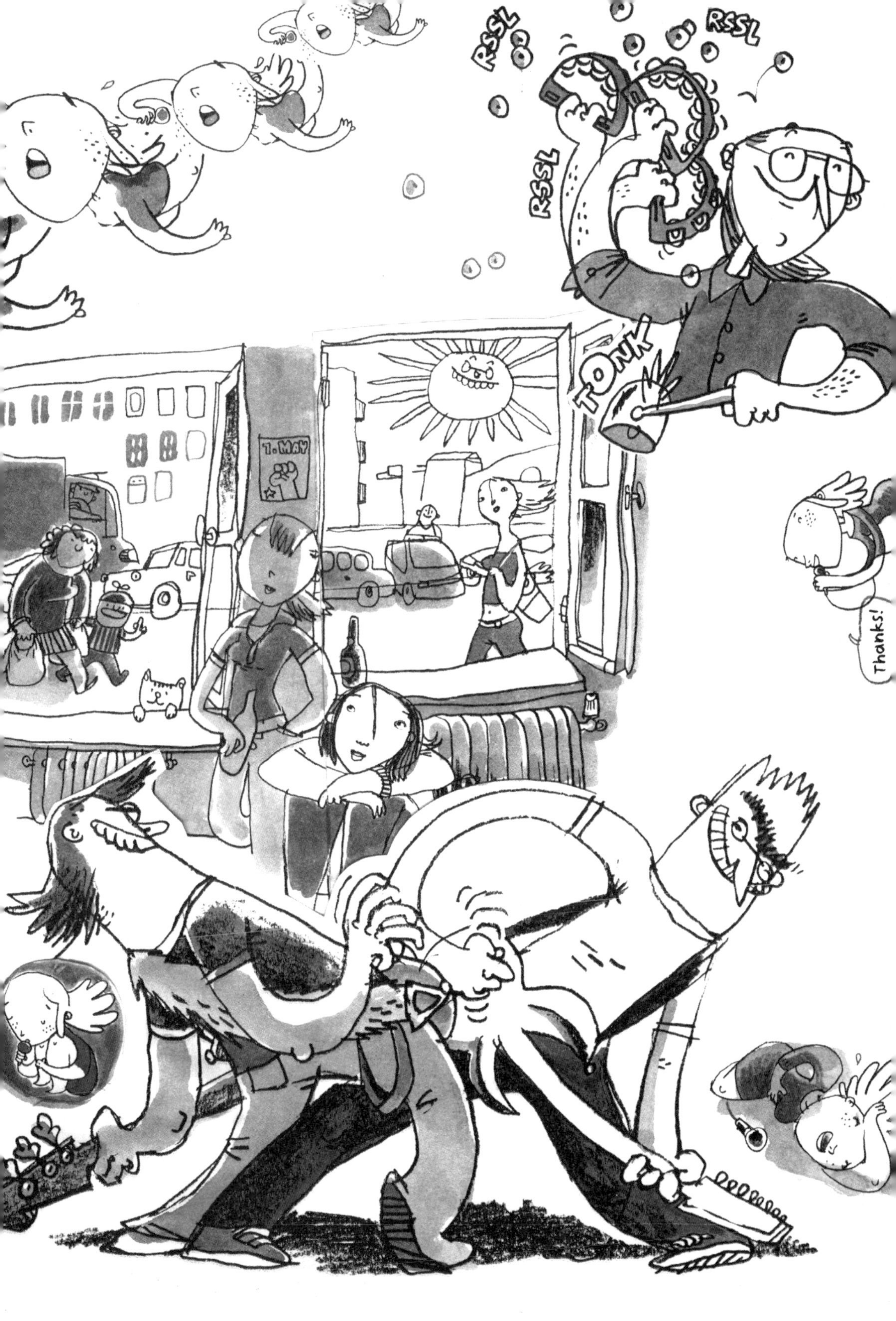
RSSL
RSSL
RSSL
TONK
1. MAY
Thanks!

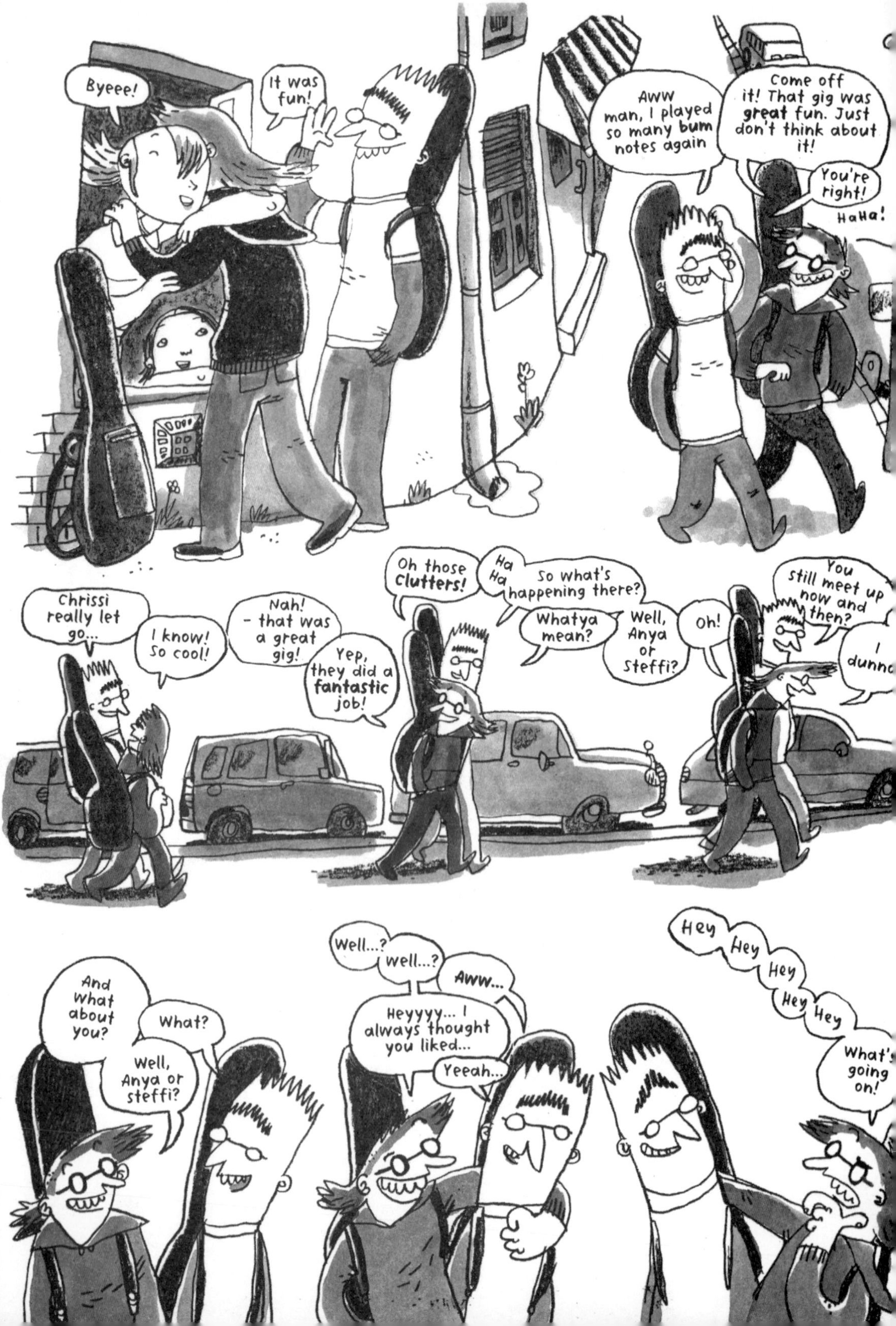

Byeee!
It was fun!
AWW man, I played so many bum notes again
Come off it! That gig was great fun. Just don't think about it!
You're right!
HaHa!
Chrissi really let go...
I know! So cool!
Nah! - that was a great gig!
Yep, they did a fantastic job!
Oh those Clutters!
Ha Ha
So what's happening there?
Whatya mean?
Well, Anya or Steffi?
Oh!
You still meet up now and then?
I dunno
And what about you?
What?
Well, Anya or Steffi?
Well...?
well...?
AWW...
Heyyyy... I always thought you liked...
Yeeah...
Hey
Hey
Hey
Hey
Hey
What's going on!

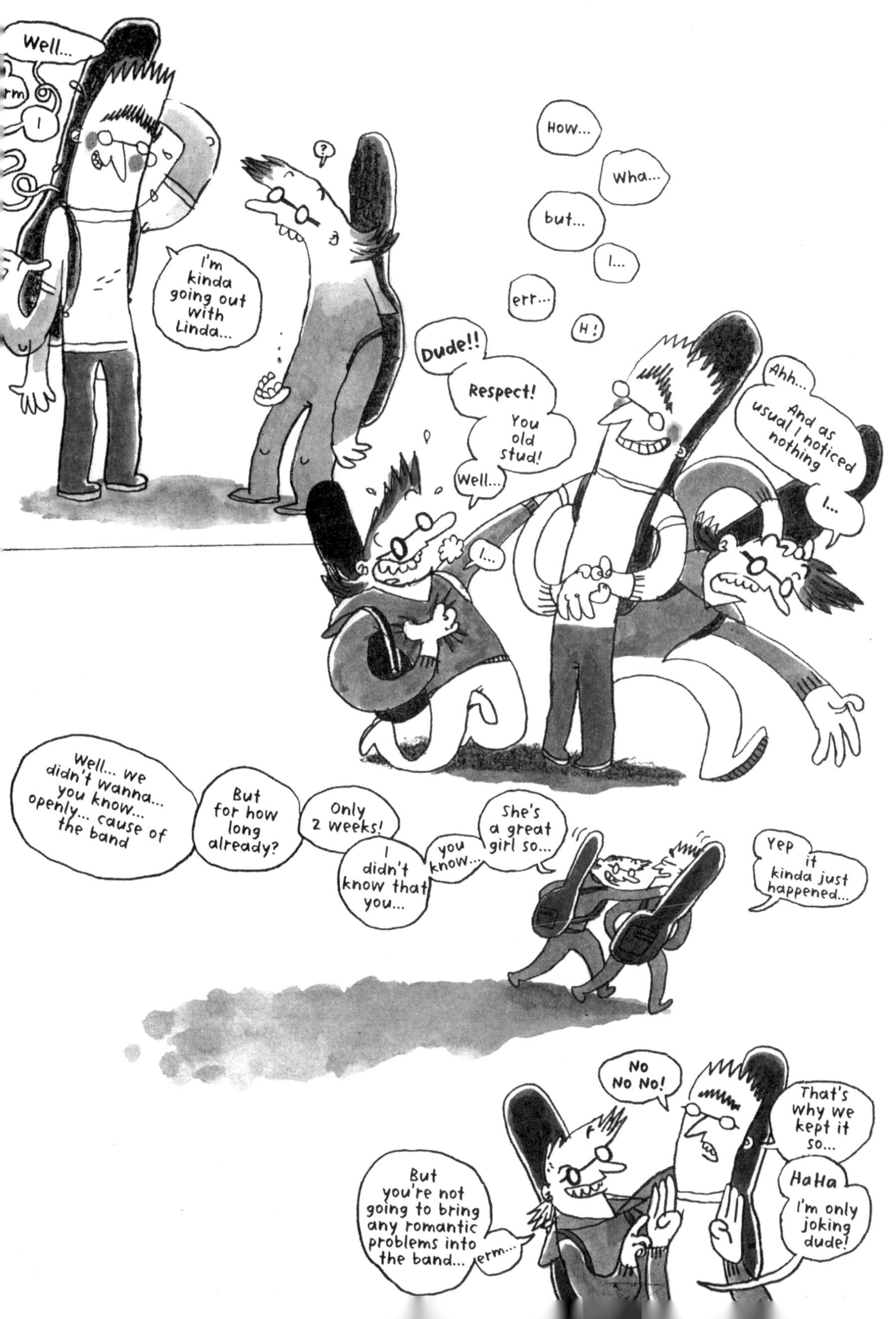

Well...
erm
I
I'm kinda going out with Linda...
?
How...
Wha...
but...
I...
err...
H!
Dude!!
Respect!
You old stud!
Well...
I...
Ahh...
And as usual I noticed nothing
I...
Well... we didn't wanna... you know... openly... cause of the band
But for how long already?
Only 2 weeks!
I didn't know that you...
you know...
She's a great girl so...
Yep it kinda just happened...
No No No!
That's why we kept it so...
HaHa I'm only joking dude!
But you're not going to bring any romantic problems into the band...
erm...

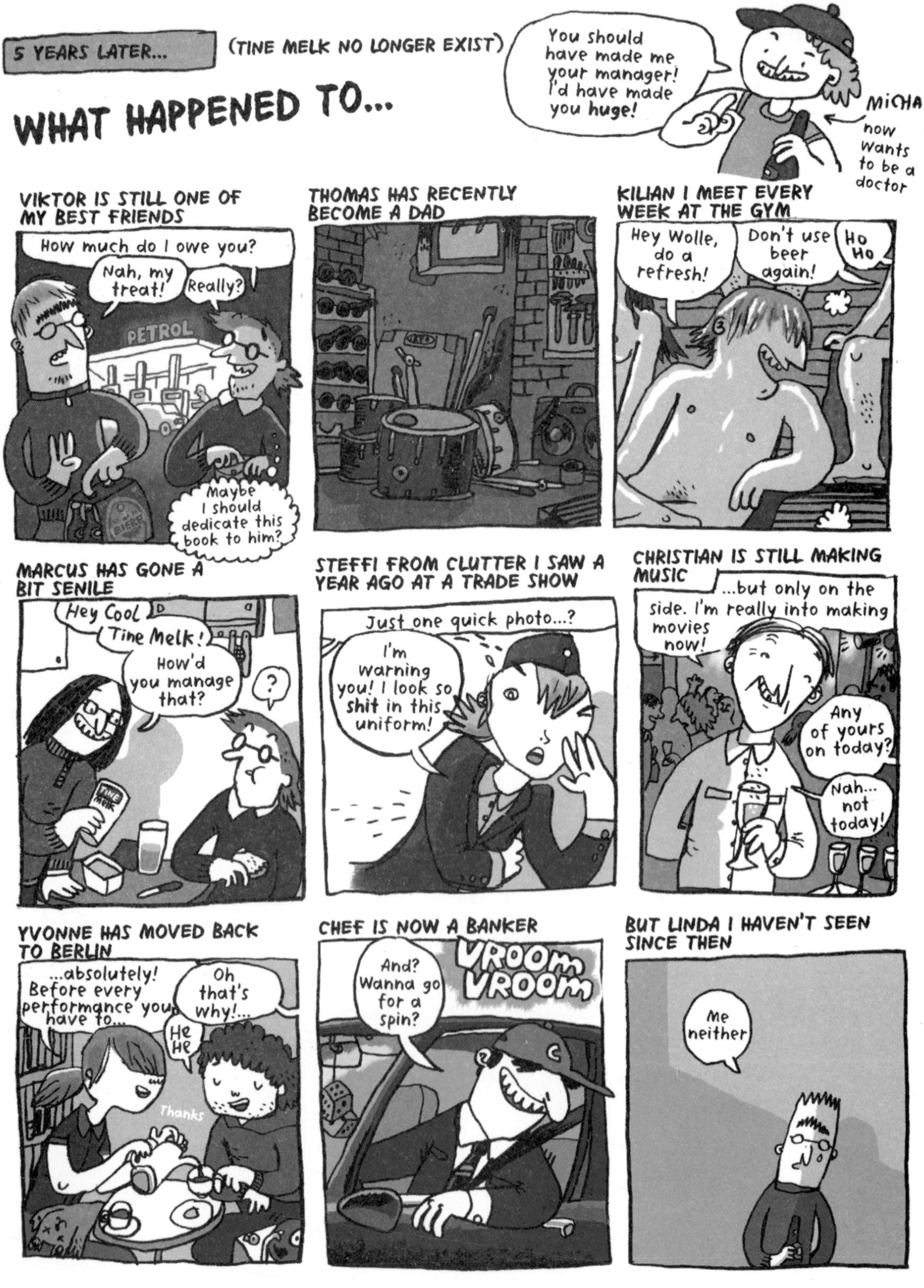
5 YEARS LATER...
(TINE MELK NO LONGER EXIST)
WHAT HAPPENED TO...
You should have made me your manager! I'd have made you huge!
MICHA now wants to be a doctor
VIKTOR IS STILL ONE OF MY BEST FRIENDS
How much do I owe you?
Nah, my treat!
Really?
PETROL
Maybe I should dedicate this book to him?
THOMAS HAS RECENTLY BECOME A DAD
KILIAN I MEET EVERY WEEK AT THE GYM
Hey Wolle, do a refresh!
Don't use beer again!
Ho Ho
MARCUS HAS GONE A BIT SENILE
Hey Cool Tine Melk!
How'd you manage that?
?
STEFFI FROM CLUTTER I SAW A YEAR AGO AT A TRADE SHOW
Just one quick photo...?
I'm warning you! I look so shit in this uniform!
CHRISTIAN IS STILL MAKING MUSIC
...but only on the side. I'm really into making movies now!
Any of yours on today?
Nah... not today!
YVONNE HAS MOVED BACK TO BERLIN
...absolutely! Before every performance you have to...
Oh that's why!...
He He
Thanks
CHEF IS NOW A BANKER
VROOM VROOM
And? Wanna go for a spin?
BUT LINDA I HAVEN'T SEEN SINCE THEN
Me neither